THE SECRET IS OUT

William Stanek is the artist behind the scenes at World Galleries, and the fiction author Robert Stanek.

BW Fall Arrives at Multnomah Falls in Canvas Print with Floating Frame

Find his art at 360 Studios

360studios.pictorem.com

williamrstanek.com

Note on Listening to Reader Feedback

At **Living Well Pathways**, our journey has always been about creating meaningful, impactful tools for personal growth. Over time, we've had the privilege of engaging with our readers—hearing your stories, learning from your insights, and understanding what truly resonates.

Your feedback has been the catalyst for this completely revised and refreshed approach. We've embraced your input, addressing the challenges you face, deepening the content, and expanding the tools to make this series even more actionable and relatable.

This updated version reflects not just our vision but also your voices. It's a testament to the power of collaboration and the shared journey toward authenticity, resilience, and purpose. Thank you for guiding us and being part of the *Living Well Pathways* evolution. Together, we're shaping a path that's as dynamic and impactful as the lives we aspire to lead.

Living Well Pathways Series Overview

Living Well Pathways represents a groundbreaking departure from traditional self-help literature. This series redefines personal development by embracing life's chaos, celebrating individuality, and providing actionable tools to navigate the complexities of modern existence. Here's what sets it apart:

Why Living Well Pathways Stands Out:

- **Authentic, No-Nonsense Approach:** Unlike traditional self-help narratives that focus on overly simplified solutions or rigid frameworks, Living Well Pathways embraces the messiness of life. It encourages readers to confront challenges directly, using chaos as a catalyst for growth instead of avoiding or masking it.
- **Active Participation Over Passive Reflection:** Where books like The Secret emphasize visualization and positivity, this series advocates for intentional action. It empowers readers to actively shape their lives, fostering resilience and self-discovery by engaging fully with life's complexities.
- **Dynamic and Evolving Purpose:** Purpose isn't static—it's a journey. Rather than offering one-size-fits-all solutions, Living Well Pathways helps readers uncover a purpose that evolves alongside their experiences, embracing uncertainty and growth.
- **Balancing Realism with Optimism:** While many personal development books focus on relentless positivity or unyielding faith, this series blends optimism with realism. It acknowledges that life includes both triumphs and struggles, teaching readers to navigate both with grace and grit.

- **Celebration of Individuality:** Rather than adhering to societal norms or traditional definitions of success, Living Well Pathways encourages readers to embrace their unique voices and chart paths that align with their core values.
- **Focus on Action and Impact:** Beyond self-reflection, this series emphasizes taking meaningful action. Readers are guided to create lasting impacts in their personal lives and communities, reinforcing that authentic living extends beyond the self.

The Living Well Pathways Series

Book 1: Chisel Your Path – Carving Authenticity and Purpose in the Chaos of Life

- **Focus:** Learn how to shape your life intentionally by cutting through distractions and uncovering your authentic self.
- **Key Themes:** Prioritization, authenticity, and navigating chaos with purpose.
- **Unique Value:** Offers practical, actionable tools to actively shape your journey, rather than merely reflecting on it.

Book 2: Harmony in the Chaos – Cultivating Balance and Resonance in Life's Symphony

- **Focus:** Achieve harmony in life's multifaceted challenges, from relationships to personal growth.
- **Key Themes:** Balancing priorities, embracing life's diversity, and cultivating meaningful connections.
- **Unique Value:** Helps readers manage life's competing demands with nuance, fostering a sense of deep balance and connection.

Book 3: Orchestrating Impact – Conducting Life's Symphony with Purpose and Resilience

- **Focus:** Discover how to lead with purpose and build resilience to make a meaningful impact in the world.
- **Key Themes:** Leadership, lasting impact, and thriving through challenges.
- **Unique Value:** Combines inspirational storytelling with strategies to create personal and societal transformation.

Single Volume: Embrace Chaos, Find Purpose

- **Comprehensive Edition:** Combines all three books, creating a cohesive guide to self-discovery, balance, and impact.
- **Exclusive Feature:** Includes The Resilient Growth Self-Assessment Tool, a $65 value, integrated into an interactive app for personalized development insights.

Who is Living Well Pathways For?

- •Those seeking authentic personal growth without the sugarcoating.
- •Individuals striving to embrace life's unpredictability and transform chaos into opportunity.
- •Readers ready to align their actions with their core values and create meaningful, lasting impact.
- •Anyone looking for practical tools and strategies to foster resilience, purpose, and balance.

Why Choose Living Well Pathways?

Living Well Pathways challenges you to reject superficial self-help clichés. It's an invitation to embrace your individuality, honor your struggles, and craft a life of authenticity and purpose. This series isn't just a guide—it's a movement toward living with intention and creating ripples of impact in the world.

Start your journey today, and discover what it means to truly live well amidst life's chaos.

Dear Seekers of Depth, Authenticity, and Meaning

In the vast, ever-shifting sea of personal growth, there lies a tapestry woven from the threads of experience, courage, and an unwavering commitment to living a life that truly resonates. This tapestry is not merely a collection of thoughts or a set of lessons—it's an offering, a guide, and an invitation to embark on a journey toward an existence that feels fully and genuinely lived.

As we explore what it means to care about what truly matters, to navigate the tangled web of priorities, and to shape our lives with intention, remember that these concepts are interconnected. They form a cohesive foundation upon which a fulfilling life is built. This book is more than just a map for personal growth; it's the essence of years spent giving careful thought, making mistakes, and savoring moments of unapologetic joy.

This isn't a typical self-help book. It's a counterpoint to the status quo, a celebration of the beautifully imperfect journey toward authenticity, and a guide for navigating the complexities of our world with resilience, flair, and an unwavering commitment to meaningful growth.

The journey of personal evolution isn't only about triumphs—it's also about responsibility. With each step toward self-discovery comes the profound duty to shape our own narrative. My own path has been one of transformation, where I've found strength in introspection and growth amid challenges. Standing at the crossroads of chaos, authenticity, and purpose, I've gathered insights that have deeply influenced my approach to living a life that matters.

Throughout my journey, I've been privileged to witness and engage in pivotal moments of personal and collective transformation—from the liberating act of saying "no" to what no longer serves us, to the joyful embrace of unapologetic authenticity. These experiences have underscored the power of personal growth, especially in times of adversity, and have reinforced my belief that real transformation transcends fleeting trends. True growth demands the courage to explore, the resilience to challenge norms, and the adaptability to navigate life's complexities.

As we embark on this journey together, I invite you to challenge conventional expectations, to venture into the uncharted territories of your true self, and to embrace the creativity and courage inherent in living authentically. May these pages serve as a guide for your own path, one that leads you to a life filled with purpose, passion, and genuine joy.

With warmest regards and encouragement,

William R. Stanek

Harmony in the Chaos: Cultivating Depth, Balance, and Resonance in Life's Symphony

Living Well Pathways, Book 2

William R. Stanek
Author & Series Creator

Harmony in the Chaos: Cultivating Depth, Balance, and Resonance in Life's Symphony

Living Well Pathways, Book 2

Published by Stanek & Associates
in conjunction with
Big Blue Sky Press for Business
www.williamrstanek.com.

2nd Edition Copyright © 2025 William R. Stanek. Seattle, Washington. All rights reserved. Photographs of the author are © HC Stanek. Fine-art photographs and illustrations are © William R. Stanek and were created by the author.

No part of this book may be reproduced, stored in a retrieval system or transmitted in any form or by any means, electronic, mechanical, photocopying, recording, scanning or otherwise, except as permitted by Sections 107 or 108 of the 1976 United States Copyright Act, without the prior written permission of the publisher Requests to the publisher for permission should be sent to the address listed previously.

Stanek & Associates is a trademark of Stanek & Associates and/or its affiliates. All other marks are the property of their respective owners. No association with any real company, organization, person or other named element is intended or should be inferred through use of company names, web site addresses or screens.

This book expresses the views and opinions of the author. The information contained in this book is provided without any express, statutory or implied warranties.

LIMIT OF LIABILITY/DISCLAIMER OF WARRANTY: THE PUBLISHER AND THE AUTHOR MAKE NO REPRESENTATIONS OR WARRANTIES WITH RESPECT TO THE ACCURACY OR COMPLETENESS OF THE CONTENTS OF THIS WORK AND SPECIFICALLY DISCLAIM ALL WARRANTIES, INCLUDING WITHOUT LIMITATION WARRANTIES OF FITNESS FOR A PARTICULAR PURPOSE. NO WARRANTY MAY BE CREATED OR EXTENDD BY SALES OR PROMOTIONAL MATERIALS. THE ADVICE AND DISCUSSION IN THIS BOOK MAY NOT BE SUITABLE FOR EVERY SITUATION. THIS WORK IS SOLD WITH THE UNDERSTANDING THTAT THE PUBLISHER IS NOT ENGAGED IN RENDERING PROFESSIONAL SERVICES AND THAT SHOULD PROFESSIONAL ASSISTANCE BE REQUIRED THE SERVICES OF A COMPETENT PROFESSIONAL SHOULD BE

SOUGHT. NEITHER THE PUBLISHERS, AUTHORS, RESELLERS NOR DISTRIBUTORS SHALL BE HELD LIABLE FOR ANY DAMAGES CAUSED OR ALLEGED TO BE CAUSE EITHER DIRECTLY OR INDIRECTLY HEREFROM. THE REFERENCE OF AN ORGANIZATION OR WEBSITE AS A SOURCE OF FURTHER INFORMATION DOES NOT MEAN THAT THE PUBLISHER OR THE AUTHOR ENDORSES THE INFORMATION THE ORGANIZATION OR WEBSITE MAY PROVIDE OR THE RECOMMENDATIONS IT MAY MAKE. FURTHER, READERS SHOULD BE AWARE THAT WEBSITES LISTED IN THIS BOOK MAY NOT BE AVAILABLE OR MAY HAVE CHANGED SINCE THIS WORK WAS WRITTEN.

Stanek & Associates publishes in a variety of formats, including print, electronic and by print-on-demand. Some materials included with standard print editions may not be included in electronic or print-on-demand editions or vice versa.

Country of First Publication: United States of America.

Cover Design: Creative Designs Ltd.
Editorial Development: Andover Publishing Solutions
Content & Technical Review: L & L Technical Content Services

You can provide feedback related to this book by emailing the author at williamstanek @ aol.com. Please use the <u>name of the book</u> as the subject line.

2nd Edition. Version: 2.1.5.1c

Stanek, William.

> **Note** I may periodically update this text and the edition and version number shown previously will let you know which version you are working with. If there's a specific feature you'd like me to write about, message me on Facebook (http://facebook.com/williamstanekauthor). Please keep in mind readership of this book determines how much time I can dedicate to it.

Table of Contents

Note on Listening to Reader Feedback 2
Living Well Pathways Series Overview 3
Dear Seekers of Depth, Authenticity, and Meaning 7
Table of Contents 15
To Seekers of Authenticity, Challengers of Convention, and Keepers of Unconventional Wisdom, ... 17
Harmony in the Chaos: Cultivating Depth, Balance, and Resonance in Life's Symphony 21
The Garden of Priorities 23
The Tapestry of Relationships 31
The Catalyst for Change 42
Beyond the Shallows 48
The Map of Purpose 59
Calibrating Your Moral Compass 69
Avoiding the Temptation of Drift 80
Storms of Distractions 89
Rogue Waves 99
Beyond the Known 106
The Art of Reflection 111
Tools of Wisdom 118
Where Purpose Thrives 124

Weathering Emotional Storms	132
Your Inner Scholar	138
Embrace Your Inner Rebel	142
Liberate Your Choices	145
The Dance of Integrity	149
The Jar of Careful Choices	153
Your Most Potent Sorcery	156
The Comfort Zone	165
The Canvas Isn't Infinite	168
The Procrastination Dragon	178
Purpose is Not a Unicorn: The Real Quest for Meaning	187
March Headlong into the Chaos	195
The Busyness Epidemic	199
The Theatre of Judgement	204
The Photoshop Rebellion	207
The Validation Revelation	211
The Eternal Now	215
4-Week Action Plan for Harmony in the Chaos: Cultivating Depth, Balance, and Resonance in Life's Symphony	225
Week 1 Action Plan: Laying Foundations for Harmony	227
Week 2 Action Plan: Deepening Connections and Embracing Change	231
Week 3 Action Plan: Embracing Integrity and Liberating Choices	235
Week 4 Action Plan: Conquering Procrastination and Embracing the Moment	239
Afterword for the Book	243
About the Author: William R. Stanek	245

To Seekers of Authenticity, Challengers of Convention, and Keepers of Unconventional Wisdom,

The journey of exploring meaningful growth and understanding what truly matters has been profound—a journey shaped by the twists, turns, and insights gained from years of navigating the unpredictable landscape of life. I want to express my deepest gratitude to those who have been part of this path with me. You are the ones who truly understand the challenges, the revisions, and the years that went into bringing this book to life.

First, my heartfelt thanks to those who have dared to question the norms—from the visionaries sharing ideas in coffee shops to the dedicated souls crafting their own paths. Your confidence in my work and your willingness to entrust me with unraveling life's complexities have been both humbling and inspiring. This book is a tribute to your courage and indomitable spirit.

To the many friends and mentors with whom I've shared this dynamic journey, thank you. Each knowing smile, every shared "What are we doing here?" moment, has contributed to the insights and perspectives that fill these pages. Your openness to embracing life's uncertainties, your defiance of convention, and your passion for innovation have all been sources of inspiration.

To my collaborators and confidants, past and present—thank you for being partners in this creative process. Your wisdom, often shared over long conversations and caffeine-fueled brainstorms, has added depth to this work. Together, we have challenged conventions, given shape to new ideas, and explored concepts that resist being confined.

Special thanks go to those who offered invaluable feedback, contributed fresh perspectives, and engaged in vibrant discussions that helped shape this book. Your unconventional ideas and commitment to thoughtful exploration are woven into every chapter. This work is as much yours as it is mine.

This book is a journey through the shared wisdom of those who have left their mark on the world—proof that real leadership is about audacious actions and meaningful impact rather than titles. It's a tribute to those who have shown that each of us holds the potential to lead with purpose, with empathy, and with a vision for positive change.

Finally, to my family—thank you for your unwavering support and patience. Your belief in me and in the purpose behind this book has been the fuel that sustained me through the process. This book carries the mark of your steadfast encouragement as much as it does my own journey.

With deepest gratitude and respect,

William R. Stanek

Harmony in the Chaos: Cultivating Depth, Balance, and Resonance in Life's Symphony

Though the chapters are crafted for brisk perusal, curb your enthusiasm from consuming the book in one go or hastily within a week. Dedicate an entire day to each chapter, diving deeply into the concepts and reflections it offers. Engage intimately with the material, truly familiarize yourself with its essence, and nurture the seeds of dissent to sprout and thrive within. This journey transcends mere reading—it's a call to waltz with your inner maverick, a methodical blueprint for unleashing the grandeur of your inherent capabilities.

The Garden of Priorities

Imagine your life as a lush, vibrant garden, and your priorities as the flowers, trees, and plants within it. Tending to this garden with intention is about cultivating an environment where your most meaningful priorities can thrive. In choosing to nurture the right things, you're making room for what truly matters to grow, allowing your garden to become a reflection of your values and dreams.

The seeds you choose to plant in this garden define what will flourish. Each seed represents a priority, a commitment, or a goal that aligns with your deeper values and aspirations. Being purposeful in what you plant means selecting priorities that support the life you wish to cultivate. Ask yourself: What do I want to see grow? Which seeds resonate with my true self? These choices create the foundation for a meaningful garden, where each bloom reflects your vision.

Just as weeds compete with flowers for space, distractions and unimportant commitments can overshadow what truly matters. Tending to your garden of priorities means removing these "weeds" with care and consistency. This is an ongoing effort to make sure that your energy goes to the right places. By pulling out distractions and unnecessary obligations, you make space for the growth of your most important priorities, ensuring they receive the light and resources they need.

In any garden, water sustains life. Similarly, emotional energy is what nurtures your priorities. Each day, you have a limited amount of energy to devote, and how you allocate it is essential to the health of your priorities. Not all areas of your life require equal attention at every moment; some may need extra care, while others can thrive with less. Being mindful of where you invest your emotional energy means nurturing the areas of your life that will most benefit from your attention and care.

Pruning is essential for any garden to thrive. It involves trimming away overgrowth or parts that no longer serve the health of the plant. In life, pruning might mean letting go of commitments, habits, or even old perspectives that no longer align with your growth. This process is not about loss but about creating space for renewal. By regularly "pruning" your life, you encourage new growth and allow your true priorities to shine.

Like a garden, our lives experience seasons—times of growth, rest, change, and renewal. In some seasons, one area of life may need more focus, while in others, a different priority will take center stage. Understanding these shifts allows you to nurture the right priorities at the right time. Embracing the seasons in your life is about respecting the natural ebb and flow, allowing your garden to adapt, renew, and stay vibrant through each phase.

A flourishing garden is rich in diversity, with various plants and flowers adding different textures, colors, and scents. In life, this means appreciating the diversity of your priorities. Each priority contributes something unique, whether it's work, family, health, or personal growth. Embracing this variety brings balance and beauty to your life, allowing you to draw meaning from each aspect of your garden.

Plants need the right balance of sunlight and shade, and your priorities need a similar balance of attention. Some areas of life thrive under constant focus, while others benefit from periods of rest. Giving attention to your priorities with this balance in mind prevents burnout and encourages steady growth. This delicate balance allows you to honor each aspect of life, contributing to a garden that is both vibrant and sustainable.

Values act as the rich, fertile soil in which your priorities grow. Just as plants need nutrients, your priorities are nourished by the values you hold. Ensuring that your actions and goals align with your core beliefs creates stability and resilience in your garden. With this solid foundation, your priorities will be more deeply rooted, better able to thrive, and less easily swayed by external pressures.

A healthy garden is protected from pests and diseases, just as your priorities need protection from negativity, self-doubt, and unnecessary outside pressures. Being vigilant against these influences means setting boundaries and protecting what matters. Guarding your priorities helps maintain a space where they can grow safely, free from forces that could weaken or undermine them.

After patient care and consistent nurturing, every garden eventually yields a harvest. In life, this harvest is the fulfillment of your goals, the satisfaction of achieving what you've worked toward. Appreciating this harvest means celebrating milestones and recognizing the progress you've made. It's a reminder of the value of intentional effort and the joy that comes from seeing your priorities flourish into meaningful achievements.

Not every flower or plant grows at the same pace, and not every priority in your life will progress at the same rate. Some goals require time and patience, while others may bloom more quickly. Recognizing and respecting these unique growth rates allows you to stay focused and motivated without rushing or forcing the process. When you honor each priority's natural timeline, you give it space to reach its fullest potential.

Pathways in a garden allow for a thoughtful journey, guiding the gardener with purpose. In life, these pathways are the plans and routines that help you move intentionally among your priorities. Setting up routines or practices to regularly engage with your priorities ensures that you stay connected to your intentions. These pathways give structure to your garden, helping you navigate your priorities with focus and clarity.

Time and attention are like water and sunlight for your priorities, essential resources for growth. In choosing where to dedicate your time, you're choosing which areas of life you want to see flourish. Allocating time to your true priorities creates a steady, reliable form of support that encourages long-term growth and stability. This intentional use of time is one of the most meaningful ways to tend to the garden of your life.

Passion is like the bees that bring life and pollination to a garden, helping it to thrive and reproduce. Inviting passion into your priorities means infusing them with enthusiasm and energy. This passion spreads, bringing vitality to every area of your life and connecting your goals with a sense of excitement and purpose. When you're passionate about what you're nurturing, you help your garden grow with a richness that lasts.

Healthy gardens have boundaries to keep out intrusions and prevent overcrowding. In life, setting boundaries around your priorities means knowing when to say "no," protecting your time, and guarding against distractions. Boundaries create a safe space where your priorities are secure and free to grow without interference. This protection is essential for your priorities to remain healthy, clear, and aligned with your values.

As a garden matures, change is a natural part of its life cycle. Some plants will fade while others come into bloom. In the same way, your priorities will evolve over time. Being open to this change allows your garden to stay relevant and fresh, growing in alignment with your shifting values and life circumstances. Embracing change means letting your garden remain dynamic, adapting to meet new seasons with grace.

A well-tended garden offers a beautiful fragrance, the reward for all the care it's been given. In life, fulfillment has a similar sweetness—the joy that comes from seeing your priorities become realities. Celebrating these moments of success and appreciating the progress you've made adds meaning to your journey. By savoring the "fragrance" of fulfillment, you create memories that remind you of the importance of nurturing what truly matters.

Each seed planted is a promise of future growth. In tending to your priorities today, you're setting the foundation for what will continue to flourish in the seasons to come. This process of planting with purpose creates a legacy, ensuring that your garden will thrive beyond today. By investing in meaningful priorities now, you prepare the soil for a life that remains rich in purpose, beauty, and growth.

In tending to the garden of priorities, you're cultivating not just a beautiful life but a purposeful one. Each flower, each plant, and each moment of care contribute to a garden that reflects the values and intentions that guide you. Let this garden be a testament to your dedication, a space that is both personally fulfilling and authentically yours.

"The Garden of Priorities" provides a framework for cultivating a life where your most significant priorities can flourish. By approaching life as a garden to be tended, you can nurture a vibrant and fulfilling existence that reflects your deepest values and aspirations that includes:

- **Intentional Planting of Priorities**   Recognize that the priorities in your life are like seeds in a garden. Choose these seeds thoughtfully, ensuring they align with your core values

and long-term aspirations. The choices you make now will determine the future blooms of your life's garden.
- **Diligent Weeding to Prevent Overcrowding**   Regularly identify and remove distractions and unnecessary commitments (weeds) that can overshadow or choke your important priorities (flowers). This continuous effort is crucial to maintain focus and clarity in your life.
- **Nurturing with Emotional Energy**   Understand that emotional energy acts like water for your garden. Wisely direct this energy to nourish the priorities that are most significant, ensuring they receive the care and attention needed to thrive.
- **Pruning for Growth and Vitality**   Engage in the practice of pruning – trimming away aspects and commitments that no longer serve your growth. This not only helps in refining your focus but also allows for new opportunities and priorities to flourish.
- **Adapting to Life's Seasons**   Be attuned to the changing seasons of your life and understand that certain priorities may ebb and flow in importance. Adapt your care and attention to these shifts to ensure a continually thriving garden.
- **Celebrating Diversity in Priorities**   Appreciate the diversity in your priorities, understanding that each one contributes uniquely to the overall beauty and balance of your life. This diversity reflects the multifaceted nature of your existence.
- **Balancing Sunlight and Shade**   Strike a delicate balance in attending to your priorities. Just like plants need both sunlight and shade, your priorities require a balanced approach to ensure healthy and sustainable growth.
- **Enriching with Values as Fertilizer**   Infuse your priorities with your core values, enriching the soil of your garden. This

alignment ensures that your priorities are deeply rooted and have the strength to flourish.
- **Guarding Against Pests of Negativity**   Stay vigilant against negative influences and doubts that can harm the health of your priorities. Protect your garden by reinforcing positive mindsets and surrounding yourself with supportive relationships.
- **Creating a Sanctuary of Priorities**   Transform your garden of priorities into a sanctuary where your most cherished aspirations and goals can safely and confidently grow. This space should feel protective, nurturing, and aligned with your true self.
- **Patiently Awaiting the Harvest**   Cultivate patience, understanding that the fruition of your priorities often takes time. Tend to your garden with care and consistency, and in time, you will enjoy the rewards of your dedicated efforts.
- **Respecting Individual Growth Rates**   Acknowledge that different priorities grow at their own pace. Some may quickly bloom, while others take longer to mature. Respect and accommodate these individual growth timelines in your nurturing approach.

The Tapestry of Relationships

Relationships, like a tapestry, are made up of countless threads woven together with intention and care. Each connection we nurture—whether family, friends, partners, or colleagues—adds its own color, texture, and meaning to our lives. Building meaningful relationships is like creating an intricate tapestry, where every bond enriches and deepens the fabric of our experiences. By investing in relationships with authenticity, respect, and empathy, we craft a tapestry that reflects the beauty and complexity of our interconnected lives.

The quality of the tapestry depends on the threads we choose. In relationships, this means focusing on connections that resonate with our values and contribute positively to our lives. Not every relationship requires the same level of commitment, but each one should hold a place of purpose. Choosing meaningful, supportive connections adds strength to your life's tapestry. These are the threads that bring true depth, resilience, and color to your relationships, creating a foundation of trust and care.

Weaving relationships is a balance of tension and harmony. Too much tension can strain and break a bond, while too little can lead to disconnect and lack of substance. Finding this balance means recognizing when to lean into growth-oriented discussions or challenges and when to weave in harmony and support. This ebb and flow create strength in the connections, allowing relationships to grow without losing stability. The delicate balance between challenge and ease is what gives relationships their depth and resilience.

The most beautiful patterns in a tapestry often come from shared values. When relationships are built on mutual respect, trust, and common beliefs, a natural pattern of alignment emerges. These shared values bring consistency and harmony, allowing connections to feel rooted and enduring. Embedding these values into the fabric of relationships strengthens the bonds and reinforces a sense of purpose, creating a tapestry that reflects a genuine alignment of principles.

Every tapestry experiences wear and tear over time, and relationships are no different. Conflicts, misunderstandings, and challenges can create small tears in even the strongest connections. Mending these moments with empathy and open communication is essential. Taking the time to understand each other's perspectives and respond with patience helps to repair rifts. This process not only restores the connection but also adds resilience and texture to the relationship, making it stronger with each repair.

Trust is the underlying structure that holds the tapestry together. Without a solid foundation of trust, even the most colorful threads will eventually come undone. Building trust requires consistent honesty, integrity, and openness. When each interaction is based on mutual trust, relationships gain stability and the freedom to grow. With this foundation, your tapestry becomes one that can withstand time and the changes life brings, providing a lasting base for the threads that make up your connections.

Relationships are created through collaboration, with each person contributing their own unique qualities, experiences, and perspectives. Recognizing the value of each person's contributions adds richness to the final design. Every interaction, gesture, and conversation weaves another strand into the tapestry, deepening the bond. Each person's individuality adds color and vibrancy, creating a shared tapestry that is uniquely reflective of both people's experiences and personalities.

Respect is a foundational pattern that runs through each thread in a healthy relationship, bringing structure and integrity to the entire tapestry. Approaching each interaction with mutual respect, even during disagreements, adds strength to the bond. This ongoing commitment to respect helps ensure that every thread is secure, making the tapestry not only more beautiful but also more durable. When respect is present in each interaction, the tapestry remains steady, even in moments of challenge.

A tapestry's strength is created thread by thread, and each connection requires consistent attention and care. Small acts of kindness, active listening, and genuine engagement build up over time to create a strong, enduring bond. Being fully present in each relationship, investing time and thought, and showing appreciation deepen the connections within the tapestry of your life. This attention to detail strengthens each bond, making the overall fabric of relationships more resilient.

Empathy is the color that brings relationships to life. Taking the time to see the world through someone else's perspective deepens each connection, creating a tapestry that is rich with understanding and compassion. Empathy allows us to feel connected to each other's joys and challenges, brightening each thread with kindness. The presence of empathy transforms relationships into a vibrant tapestry, where each person feels valued, heard, and seen.

Just as in any weaving process, knots and tangles will occasionally appear. Rather than pulling or forcing through these obstacles, patience is required to untangle them carefully. Approaching moments of tension or miscommunication with calmness allows for a smoother resolution, preserving the beauty of the relationship. The careful work of resolving issues adds durability to each connection and reinforces the strength of the tapestry as a whole.

Like a tapestry that changes with time, relationships evolve through different seasons. Some connections may grow stronger, while others may fade as priorities shift. Embracing these changes and recognizing the role that different people play during various stages of life enriches the tapestry.

Whether through times of joy, loss, or change, these seasons contribute new hues and textures, adding depth and resilience to the woven fabric of relationships.

Healthy relationships, like a well-crafted tapestry, require structure and space to thrive. Setting boundaries is essential to maintaining balance within connections. Boundaries define where each person ends and the other begins, creating a respectful space that allows for individual growth. Boundaries prevent the threads from becoming tangled, preserving the integrity of each relationship. This respectful distance allows both parties to flourish within the framework of the relationship, making it a more fulfilling experience for all involved.

Shared memories are the embellishments that make the tapestry of relationships unique and memorable. These moments become part of the fabric, reminders of shared laughter, milestones, and experiences. Creating and cherishing these memories together enriches relationships, making the tapestry more meaningful. Each memory adds a detail to the design, contributing to a sense of warmth and familiarity within the relationship.

Each person brings their own unique qualities to the tapestry, and celebrating this individuality enriches the entire design. Appreciating each person's strengths, differences, and perspectives adds texture and depth to the relationship. Just as varied threads bring richness to a woven piece, individual differences contribute to a more interesting, dynamic, and resilient tapestry. Embracing this diversity allows relationships to be authentic and full of life.

The texture of presence is what brings relationships to life. Truly showing up for others—actively listening, engaging, and being attentive—adds a tangible depth to each thread. Being fully present transforms relationships from passive connections into active, fulfilling engagements. This presence creates a tapestry that feels meaningful and complete, as each thread is woven with intention and care.

In relationships, a little tension can be a good thing. Like the tautness needed to hold woven threads together, a healthy amount of tension keeps connections lively and engaged. Recognizing when to add a little stretch, and when to relax, is a skill that helps relationships grow stronger without becoming strained. This adaptability keeps the tapestry flexible, allowing for the natural expansion and strengthening of each bond.

Vulnerability is what allows connections to deepen and grow. When we share openly and honestly with others, we add authenticity and strength to each relationship. Embracing vulnerability allows relationships to feel real and grounded, giving each thread a richness that adds depth to the tapestry. Openness and trust allow relationships to move beyond the surface, fostering genuine intimacy and connection.

Over time, threads may fray, and forgiveness is the needle that can mend them. Recognizing that mistakes and misunderstandings are part of any relationship allows us to forgive and repair, rather than discard or disconnect. Forgiveness strengthens bonds and restores the integrity of the tapestry, ensuring that small rips don't become larger tears. This practice of repair allows relationships to heal and grow stronger over time.

Shared dreams are the grand designs that give direction and vision to the tapestry. Relationships that embrace a shared purpose or vision allow each person to invest in something larger than themselves. These shared dreams unite individuals, bringing a sense of excitement and purpose to the relationship. The threads of shared aspirations add a unifying design to the tapestry, inspiring both people to work together toward meaningful goals.

A tapestry is rarely ever complete, and the beauty of relationships lies in their ongoing evolution. Each day, we add new threads, make repairs, and weave new patterns. Embracing the unfinished nature of relationships allows us to see the beauty in progress, celebrating the journey rather than focusing only on the outcome. This openness to continuous growth and change makes the tapestry of relationships richer, more resilient, and filled with possibility.

In weaving this tapestry of relationships, you create a life filled with color, connection, and meaning. Each thread, woven with care and purpose, contributes to a life that reflects the values and love you bring to the world. Let your relationships be a true testament to the depth, beauty, and fulfillment that come from nurturing connections with intention and respect.

The Loom of Life

Imagine relationships as the loom of life, where each thread represents a bond you've nurtured. Some threads are vibrant and bold, adding vitality and excitement. Others are softer, offering comfort and stability. Every connection contributes to the larger design of your life—a unique and intricate tapestry that reflects your journey. The question is: how do we choose, care for, and strengthen these threads so our tapestry remains resilient and beautiful?

The "WEAVE" Framework for Relationship Building

Use the "WEAVE" method to cultivate meaningful relationships:

1. **W – Welcome Authenticity:** Show up as your true self and encourage others to do the same. Authenticity is the foundation of trust.
2. **E – Empathy in Action:** Practice active listening and respond with compassion. This brings vibrancy to your relationships.
3. **A – Align Values:** Focus on connections that share common values to ensure enduring bonds.
4. **V – Value Differences:** Embrace the diversity of each thread, as it adds texture and richness to the tapestry.
5. **E – Evolve Together:** Allow your relationships to grow and adapt, honoring the changes in both yourself and others.

Repairing Tears: The 3R Approach

When conflicts arise, use the "3R Approach" to mend and strengthen bonds:

1. **Reflect:** Take time to understand the source of the tension or misunderstanding.
2. **Reach Out:** Approach the other person with openness, seeking resolution rather than blame.
3. **Reinforce:** Strengthen the relationship with actions that rebuild trust, such as affirmations, apologies, or shared experiences.

Think of your relationships as a symphony, where each connection plays a different instrument. Some are percussion, adding rhythm and drive, while others are strings, bringing melody and warmth. Together, they create a harmony that defines your life. Miscommunication is like a discordant note—temporary but fixable with attention and care.

Knots in your tapestry are like life's challenges—they can be frustrating, but they also hold the threads in place. Learning to untangle them carefully, rather than cutting them out, ensures the integrity of the design remains intact.

Journaling Prompts: Threads of Connection
- What relationships in your life add the most color and depth to your tapestry?
- Reflect on a time when a bond was strengthened through conflict resolution. What did you learn from the experience?
- Which threads in your tapestry need more attention, and how can you nurture them intentionally?

Visualization Exercise: Crafting Your Tapestry
- Close your eyes and imagine your life as a tapestry. Visualize the threads that represent your closest relationships. What colors do they have? Are there any frayed edges or knots? Picture yourself carefully weaving new threads, repairing tears, and adding bright, vibrant strands. Feel the strength and beauty of your tapestry growing under your care.

Shift your perspective from seeing relationships as transactions—what you give versus what you get—to transformations, where every interaction is an opportunity for growth and connection. Relationships flourish when they are viewed as spaces for mutual enrichment, not obligations.

Recognize that no tapestry is flawless. The imperfections in your relationships—the disagreements, the moments of distance—add authenticity and character. These are the marks of a life lived with vulnerability and courage.

Action Plans and Strategies

The Thread-by-Thread Approach

1. **Daily Presence:** Dedicate time each day to meaningful connections—whether it's a phone call, a message, or a heartfelt conversation.
2. **Acts of Kindness:** Small, consistent gestures like a note of appreciation or a listening ear create strong threads over time.
3. **Shared Experiences:** Plan activities that build memories, such as trying a new hobby together or revisiting a cherished tradition.

Boundaries: The Frame of the Tapestry

- Identify areas where boundaries are needed to prevent entanglement or overcommitment.
- Practice communicating boundaries respectfully, ensuring both parties feel valued.
- Review and adjust boundaries as relationships evolve, maintaining balance and respect.

Every thread you weave is a testament to your care and intention. Celebrate the relationships that bring you joy, challenge you to grow, and provide unwavering support. These connections are the colors of your life, making your tapestry vibrant and meaningful. With each thread, you craft a legacy of love, resilience, and connection—a masterpiece uniquely your own.

The most beautiful tapestries are not those without knots or flaws, but those woven with care, courage, and creativity. Embrace the threads of your relationships, for they are the fabric of your life.

The Catalyst for Change

Passion ignites the inner fire of purpose, bringing energy and meaning to all we do. True passion—the kind that aligns with our deepest values—has the power to shape lives, drive purposeful action, and inspire change. Embracing passion as a catalyst for growth and transformation means tapping into this energy with intention, allowing it to guide and fuel us. When we devote ourselves to what we genuinely care about, our lives gain direction, resilience, and a sense of fulfillment.

Passion is the spark that lights the furnace of purpose, transforming abstract goals into meaningful pursuits. When you allow yourself to pursue what truly matters, you're igniting this fire within, setting your intentions ablaze with clarity and direction. This passion doesn't just illuminate your own path; it becomes a beacon for others, showing that a life driven by purpose has a vitality all its own.

When fueled by passion, even the most routine actions become infused with meaning. Passionate engagement has a transformative effect, turning ordinary experiences into moments of discovery, joy, and growth. This approach to life brings depth to our days, as every task, big or small, becomes an opportunity to bring our best selves forward. Choosing to engage with passion allows you to experience life with a heightened sense of purpose, where enthusiasm enhances each experience and adds value to every endeavor.

Passion is the energy behind change; it motivates us to seek, create, and implement transformations in ourselves and in the world. When aligned with values, passion becomes a powerful driver of positive impact, channeling your energy toward causes and initiatives that matter. Whether in personal growth or social change, allowing passion to lead you means using this inner fire to shape a life of purpose and progress, one that's aligned with your most cherished beliefs.

True passion reveals our authentic selves. When you follow what you genuinely care about, you express your unique voice, embodying the values that matter most. This authenticity is powerful—it inspires a life that is unapologetically true to who you are. Living with this sincerity creates a sense of alignment, allowing your passions to shape an existence that feels natural, grounded, and genuinely meaningful.

Enthusiasm is the energy that forges connections, bringing people together in ways that are both joyful and resilient.

When we approach relationships with genuine enthusiasm, we create bonds rooted in shared values and mutual encouragement. This enthusiasm allows for connections that stand the test of time, grounded in an energy that goes beyond fleeting interests. Relationships built on shared passion are lasting ones, and they bring a richness to life that grows with every encounter.

Passion has a unique way of transforming challenges into meaningful growth opportunities. When we approach obstacles with a passionate resolve, they become stepping stones rather than barriers. The process of overcoming challenges fuels personal and collective growth, teaching us resilience and opening doors to new insights. Embracing challenges with passion allows you to grow stronger and wiser, adding depth to your journey and empowering you to move forward with purpose.

Passion is contagious. When you live with a strong sense of purpose, you inspire others to pursue their own dreams and passions. Empowering those around you with this energy can create a ripple effect, inspiring growth, courage, and ambition in others. Living with this enthusiasm doesn't just enrich your life; it has the power to uplift and encourage the people around you to realize their own potential.

Passion fuels emotional resilience, giving you strength and determination in the face of challenges. When you're invested in what truly matters, setbacks become easier to navigate, as your commitment to your purpose helps you persevere. This resilience creates a shield against the adversities of life, keeping you grounded and steady as you move through each experience. Embracing passion as a source of resilience means living with a sense of inner strength, capable of weathering life's storms.

Passion is often the muse behind creativity and innovation. When we care deeply about something, our minds open to new possibilities, leading us to solutions and ideas we might not have considered otherwise. By tapping into this passion, you allow creativity to flow freely, enriching your work and personal pursuits. This wellspring of ideas and inspiration fuels innovative thinking, creating possibilities that can make a lasting impact.

Passion is the source of sustained motivation, an inner fire that propels us forward. Keeping this flame alive means regularly engaging with what inspires you, stoking the embers of purpose so that they continue to light your path. When you live with a deep sense of purpose, motivation becomes a constant companion, energizing you to take each step with confidence and excitement. This sustained passion is the driving force that keeps you moving toward your goals, no matter the challenges.

Passion helps us shape a purposeful life, like a sculptor chipping away to reveal a masterpiece. Following what you're passionate about helps remove distractions and unnecessary pursuits, allowing you to focus on what truly matters. By consistently engaging with your passions, you create a life that reflects your values, revealing a sense of purpose that is clear, genuine, and aligned with your deepest goals.

Time devoted to pursuing what matters is always time well spent. Whether in work, relationships, or personal development, dedicating time to what you're passionate about enriches your life and brings lasting satisfaction. Understanding this makes it easier to prioritize meaningful pursuits over fleeting distractions, allowing you to cultivate a life that is fulfilling and rewarding.

Passion has the power to elevate everyday tasks into sources of joy, creativity, and fulfillment. When you approach even the simplest of actions with enthusiasm, you add purpose to your daily life. The mundane becomes meaningful, and routine tasks offer moments of creativity and engagement. By living with passion, you bring color and vibrancy to all you do, transforming your life into an experience filled with depth and purpose.

Passion fuels intentional action, helping you live with a sense of purpose and clarity. When each step is guided by what genuinely inspires you, your actions become deliberate and impactful. Living with intention means not only pursuing personal growth but also contributing positively to others. Passionate, intentional action creates a ripple effect, influencing those around you and contributing to a life that is meaningful and filled with purpose.

In embracing passion as the catalyst for change, you're choosing to live a life that is active, inspired, and aligned with what matters most. Each day becomes an opportunity to engage deeply, create meaning, and move with purpose. This journey—one fueled by passion—is one of continual growth, empowerment, and fulfillment, leading to a life that is vibrant, resilient, and profoundly authentic.

Passion is more than a fleeting emotion; it is a compass guiding the journey of self-discovery. Truly caring about what matters means embracing the alchemy of self-discovery through passionate pursuits, allowing your interests and curiosities to illuminate the path toward a deeper understanding of your authentic self.

- **Passion Amplifies Impact:** Passion is the force multiplier for meaningful contribution. Caring about what matters means understanding the transformative power of passion, recognizing how your devoted efforts can create ripples of positive change far beyond your immediate surroundings.
- **From Seed to Fulfillment:** Passion is the seed that grows into the flourishing tree of fulfillment. Caring deeply involves intentionally cultivating this seed, tending to it with focus and purpose until it blossoms into a vibrant, fulfilling landscape of purpose and satisfaction.
- **Fearless Pursuit:** Passion fuels bold and fearless action. Caring about what matters means channeling your passion as the driving force that propels you beyond fear and self-doubt, enabling you to transcend limitations and pursue your dreams with courage and conviction.

Endurance takes on new meaning when infused with the alchemy of passion. Truly caring about what matters means transforming challenges into stepping stones, allowing your passion to bring joy to the process. Through this lens, obstacles become opportunities for growth, and perseverance becomes a joyful celebration of progress and purpose.

By aligning your actions with your passions, you not only uncover the depths of your potential but also create a life of meaningful contribution, fulfillment, and fearless pursuit of what truly matters.

Beyond the Shallows

Beyond the shallow waters of routine and superficiality lies a vast, uncharted ocean, an expanse where depth and meaning await those who are willing to explore. Embracing what truly matters requires the courage to dive into this abyss, to venture beyond the surface and discover the hidden layers of life, self, and connection. In these deeper waters, where distractions fall away, we encounter clarity, purpose, and a sense of profound fulfillment.

In the depths, you uncover facets of yourself that remain hidden in the shallows. By exploring beyond the surface, you encounter aspects of your identity that hold richness and complexity—parts that may have been obscured or forgotten.

Delving into these deeper layers requires courage and curiosity, but the rewards are immense: a greater understanding of who you are, a clearer sense of purpose, and a stronger connection to your values.

Surface-level connections lack the substance that gives relationships meaning and resilience. True connection comes from investing time, empathy, and understanding in others, fostering bonds that go beyond superficial exchanges. Building these deeper connections allows for genuine empathy and mutual respect, creating relationships that can weather life's ups and downs. When you commit to nurturing this depth, you forge relationships that become a true source of support, joy, and insight.

Shallow pursuits offer fleeting satisfaction but rarely contribute to lasting fulfillment. Engaging with depth means moving beyond trivial distractions and focusing on endeavors that carry significance. This redirection of energy allows you to invest in pursuits aligned with your values and long-term goals, giving your time and efforts lasting impact. Letting go of shallow diversions brings clarity, helping you engage with what brings meaning and growth to your life.

Values are the bedrock beneath the waves, the principles that support and guide you as you navigate life's depths. Understanding and nurturing these values provides a foundation that gives strength to your decisions and direction to your actions. In exploring this inner core, you develop a sense of clarity and purpose that grounds you, enabling you to make choices that resonate with who you truly are.

In the quiet of the depths, your true passions reveal themselves, free from the distractions of surface life. These are the pursuits that resonate with the deepest parts of your being, sparking genuine enthusiasm and commitment. Exploring these passions adds purpose to your life, allowing you to engage in activities that fulfill and sustain you. By bringing these passions to light, you create a life that is not only meaningful but also filled with joy and energy.

Purpose thrives in the deep waters of significance. When you move beyond the shallows of aimless pursuits, you find a direction that feels true to your core. Purpose is not something to be found on the surface; it often requires exploration and introspection. By venturing into these depths, you can identify the currents that lead you toward a meaningful existence, helping you avoid the aimless drift of shallow living.

Growth flourishes in the depths, where experiences have the power to shape and refine us. When you immerse yourself in the challenges and opportunities of life, you grow stronger, more resilient, and more self-aware. Allowing yourself to learn from both successes and setbacks enriches your character, fostering an evolution that can only come from transformative experiences. In these depths, growth is a lifelong journey, a continuous process of becoming.

Authenticity is found in the profound waters, where societal expectations and superficial facades dissolve. In the depths, you're free to express your truest self, unencumbered by external pressures. This resonance with authenticity allows you to live a life that feels real and aligned, where your actions and words mirror your inner values. Authenticity in these deep waters provides a sense of peace and fulfillment that can only come from living genuinely.

Empathy is a rare treasure, discovered only when we look beyond the surface. In exploring the experiences and emotions of others, we develop a profound understanding that goes beyond sympathy. By diving into empathy, you create connections built on genuine understanding and compassion, fostering a world where each person's unique journey is valued. This depth of empathy brings us closer to others, creating bonds of support, trust, and mutual respect.

The search for validation is often noisy in the shallows, where external approval is highly valued. But in the depths, you discover a more stable source of validation—one rooted in your own values and actions. By finding confidence in the authenticity of your choices, you no longer depend on external approval. Instead, you gain self-assurance from knowing that your life aligns with your beliefs, allowing you to find peace and contentment from within.

True meaning exists in the deep waters of life, where we explore relationships, work, and contributions with intention. This search for meaning is a journey that requires patience, curiosity, and commitment, guiding you to connect with what truly matters. When you seek meaning in the depths, your life gains a richness and purpose that no surface-level pursuit can offer. Meaning becomes the guiding force that brings coherence and depth to all you do.

In the profound ocean of existence, there is a balance between darkness and light, joy and sorrow. Accepting both sides of life's complexities allows you to experience life fully, recognizing that true understanding comes from embracing every facet. In these deeper waters, you learn to navigate life's nuances, appreciating the depth and richness that emerge from its complexity.

The shallows may be filled with noise and distraction, but the depths offer silence and introspection. In this quiet, you find the space to reflect, listen, and connect with your innermost thoughts. This silence is a source of peace, a sanctuary where you can reconnect with your purpose and align yourself with what truly matters. Embracing this stillness provides clarity and strength, creating a calm center in the midst of life's demands.

Shallow connections may come easily, but authentic relationships are built in the depths. By investing time, honesty, and vulnerability, you create relationships that are grounded in understanding and mutual respect. These connections, shaped by the tides of genuine care, have the resilience to withstand challenges and the capacity to grow over time. They are the relationships that enrich life, offering companionship, trust, and support.

In the depths, you encounter your true self, free from the distractions and influences that often mask your identity. This journey of self-discovery involves confronting both your strengths and weaknesses, revealing the full dimensions of who you are. As you peel away layers of pretense, you gain insight into your character, allowing you to live with a sense of self-awareness and confidence that comes only from true understanding.

While the storms in the shallows are fleeting, those in the depths carry more weight and can transform us. Enduring these challenges builds resilience, shaping you into a stronger, wiser individual. By navigating life's difficulties with courage and openness, you gain the tools to face future obstacles with grace. These experiences teach you that growth often comes from adversity, and that the depths hold the potential for profound transformation.

Purpose can become obscured in the shallows, where distractions and temporary goals pull us in different directions. When you dive into the depths, you bring purpose to the surface, allowing it to guide your journey. This clarity of purpose ensures that your actions and decisions are aligned with what you value most, bringing direction and meaning to your life.

In the depths, each experience yields pearls of wisdom, small yet invaluable insights gained from a life lived with purpose and reflection. These insights, often hard-won, enrich your understanding and add layers of meaning to your life. Treasuring these "pearls" allows you to build a life that is both insightful and impactful, one where every experience, whether joyful or challenging, contributes to your personal growth.

The depths offer a space where intentions are clarified and refined, allowing you to act with genuine purpose. By aligning your actions with your values, you ensure that each step you take is meaningful and intentional. This clarity strengthens your commitment to what truly matters, allowing you to live a life guided by integrity and purpose.

In choosing to move beyond the shallows and explore the depths, you are engaging in a journey of self-discovery, resilience, and profound meaning. Here, life is richer, relationships are stronger, and purpose is clear. These deeper waters hold the promise of a life lived fully, where each moment is a part of a larger journey toward fulfillment, authenticity, and enduring growth. Embrace this depth, and you will find that beneath the surface lies a world of significance, waiting to be explored.

Living Deeply

Living deeply is not an occasional act; it's a way of being. It means bringing intention, presence, and authenticity to every aspect of life. Beyond the shallows of superficial engagement lies a profound commitment to aligning your thoughts, actions, and relationships with your core values. This chapter explores the practices and principles that empower you to cultivate depth, allowing every moment to resonate with purpose and meaning.

1. The Call to Depth

Living deeply begins with a choice—the decision to turn away from distractions and engage fully with the richness of life. This choice requires courage and intention, as the pull of the shallows is ever-present. Answering the call to depth means embracing vulnerability, curiosity, and the willingness to grow.

Reflective Question: What areas of my life are currently in the shallows, and how can I bring more depth to them?

2. The Practice of Presence

Depth thrives in the now. Living deeply requires cultivating presence, where each moment is approached with undivided attention. Whether it's a conversation, a meal, or a creative pursuit, being fully present transforms ordinary activities into extraordinary experiences.

Practice: Mindful Engagement: Choose one daily task—washing dishes, drinking coffee, or walking—and perform it mindfully. Notice every detail, from the sensations to your emotions, as you engage fully in the present.

3. Aligning with Core Values

Living deeply means living in alignment with your values. These are the principles that ground you and provide direction in the midst of life's complexities. By reflecting on your values, you create a foundation that supports meaningful decisions and actions.

Exercise: Value Inventory: Write down your top five values. Reflect on how your daily choices align with them. Identify one action you can take this week to bring your life closer to your core principles.

4. The Depth of Connection

Depth in relationships comes from investing time, empathy, and vulnerability. It's about moving beyond transactional exchanges to build bonds rooted in mutual respect and genuine understanding.

Practice: Deep Listening: In your next conversation, listen without interrupting or planning your response. Focus entirely on understanding the other person's perspective. Reflect on how this deepens your connection.

5. Meaningful Pursuits

The pursuit of depth requires choosing activities and goals that align with your passions and purpose. This means letting go of trivial distractions and dedicating your energy to endeavors that resonate deeply with your authentic self.

Exercise: The Depth Audit: Review how you currently spend your time. Categorize your activities as "Shallow" (surface-level or draining) or "Deep" (fulfilling and purposeful). Adjust your schedule to prioritize deep pursuits.

6. Resilience in the Depths

Life's storms are more profound in the depths, but they also offer opportunities for growth and transformation. Building resilience means embracing challenges as catalysts for self-discovery and strength.

Practice: The Growth Lens: Reflect on a recent challenge. Ask yourself: What did this teach me? How did it help me grow? Use this perspective to reframe future difficulties as opportunities for evolution.

7. Authenticity as a Compass

Authenticity is the guiding star of a life lived deeply. By embracing who you truly are, you free yourself from the expectations of others and create a life that reflects your inner truth.

Exercise: The Authentic Action: Identify one area where you feel pressured to conform. Commit to a small action that aligns with your authentic self, whether it's expressing a preference, pursuing a passion, or setting a boundary.

8. Embracing Complexity

Depth means accepting the full spectrum of human experience—joy and sorrow, success and failure. By embracing life's complexities, you cultivate a resilience that allows you to navigate challenges with grace and gratitude.

Practice: The Duality Journal: At the end of each day, write down one moment of joy and one challenge. Reflect on how each contributed to your growth and understanding of life's richness.

9. The Power of Silence

In the depths, silence is not empty—it is full of insight and clarity. Creating moments of quiet allows you to reconnect with yourself and your purpose, providing a calm center amidst life's demands.

Practice: Daily Stillness: Dedicate five minutes each day to silence. Sit quietly, breathe deeply, and simply observe your thoughts without judgment. Use this time to ground yourself and reset your focus.

10. The Legacy of Depth

Living deeply is not just about the present—it's about creating a life that leaves a meaningful legacy. By aligning your actions with your purpose and values, you build a life that inspires and impacts others.

Reflective Question: What do I want to be remembered for? How can I begin living that legacy today?

Living Deeply: A Daily Commitment

Depth is not a destination; it's a practice. It's the way you show up for yourself and others, the way you engage with your passions, and the way you navigate life's challenges. By committing to living deeply, you transform every aspect of your existence into an expression of authenticity and purpose.

The Map of Purpose

Purpose is a map guiding us through the varied landscapes of life. Living with intention means charting a path that aligns with our core values, convictions, and aspirations. This map isn't a rigid, predetermined route but a dynamic framework that evolves as we grow, serving as both compass and canvas. By aligning our actions with purpose, we move beyond momentary fulfillment, crafting a life rich in meaning, depth, and impact.

The map of purpose is an intentional creation, one that we draw and adjust as we move through life. Aligning our choices with a sense of purpose is a deliberate act that guides us away from distractions and toward meaningful goals. This clarity is what turns the everyday into a purposeful journey, allowing us to approach each decision with a commitment to what truly matters.

Along the journey, certain moments, relationships, and experiences stand out as waypoints—significant markers that reflect our values and contribute to the story of our lives. Recognizing these waypoints allows us to appreciate the depth they add, helping us understand the broader purpose we're moving toward. These waypoints, whether challenges, achievements, or quiet realizations, are the milestones that enrich our journey and mark our growth.

Authenticity is a key landmark on the map of purpose. In a world that often rewards conformity, staying true to oneself can be a powerful act. Living authentically means making choices that reflect our values, not what is expected or easy. This dedication to being genuine serves as a guidepost, keeping us aligned with our purpose, no matter the pressures to follow others' paths.

Conviction acts as the compass on the map of purpose, pointing us toward the true north of our principles. When we follow this internal compass, we make choices grounded in our beliefs rather than swayed by external influences. This steadfastness offers direction and confidence, helping us remain centered on our purposeful path, even when faced with the allure of short-term gratification or convenience.

The path of purpose has its share of distractions—places that consume our time and energy without providing meaningful value. These "swamps" can pull us off course, draining focus and diverting us from what we truly care about. Skillfully navigating around these diversions allows us to stay on the purposeful path, ensuring that our resources are directed toward pursuits that align with our values and goals.

Life's map features peaks of fulfillment—moments of deep satisfaction and achievement that reflect our dedication to purpose. These peaks remind us that meaningful goals require effort and perseverance. The journey up these mountains can be challenging, but reaching these heights offers a perspective and sense of accomplishment that make the climb worthwhile. These summits represent moments when we feel truly aligned, a testament to our journey's purpose.

On the map of purpose, valleys of challenge are inevitable. Rather than seeing these low points as setbacks, we can view them as essential parts of our growth. Challenges test our resilience and commitment, shaping our character and deepening our understanding of our purpose. Moving through these valleys with openness allows us to emerge stronger and more capable, turning obstacles into opportunities for meaningful growth.

Throughout our journey, we encounter people who share our values and vision. These purposeful companions are those who support, inspire, and encourage us. Building relationships with like-minded individuals amplifies our impact and creates a sense of community. Together, we can achieve more, collaborating and uplifting each other as we move forward on our purposeful paths.

The map of purpose includes unknown territories, areas that invite curiosity and courage. Exploring these new realms helps us grow, discover, and expand our understanding of what's possible. Embracing these uncharted territories opens us up to unexpected opportunities, adding richness to our journey and allowing us to grow beyond the boundaries we once thought defined us.

Purpose isn't static. Just as we grow, our understanding of purpose deepens and changes. Staying open to this evolution means recognizing when it's time to recalibrate our direction. As life unfolds, we may find that our map needs updating to reflect our current beliefs and aspirations. Embracing this adaptability keeps us aligned with our purpose, allowing our journey to remain authentic and meaningful.

Crossroads present moments of decision, where our choices define the course of our journey. Standing at these intersections with purpose means choosing paths that align with our values, even when easier options might tempt us. Each choice we make at a crossroads shapes the direction of our lives, reinforcing our commitment to a purpose-driven existence.

Values are the North Star on our map, a constant that provides guidance even in uncertain times. By aligning our actions with these core beliefs, we ensure that our journey remains authentic and true to who we are. This unwavering dedication to values gives us direction and purpose, illuminating our path even when the destination seems distant.

The map of purpose includes forests of temptation—places that offer instant gratification but ultimately divert us from our path. Navigating these distractions with discipline allows us to stay focused on long-term fulfillment rather than short-term satisfaction. By staying true to our purpose, we build resilience, avoiding detours that may take us off track.

Rivers of passion flow through the landscape of purpose, carrying us toward pursuits that energize and inspire us. Embracing this enthusiasm allows us to infuse our journey with creativity, dedication, and joy. When we align our actions with what we're passionate about, we create momentum, moving with a sense of vitality and engagement that makes each step meaningful.

Bridges of connection allow us to cross divides, fostering relationships with others who share our purpose. These bridges create networks of support, collaboration, and shared ambition, amplifying the impact of our efforts. By connecting with others who are on similar journeys, we strengthen our own path, gaining encouragement and perspective that enrich our experience.

In the toolkit of purpose, self-reflection is an essential instrument. Regularly assessing our choices, motivations, and progress helps us stay on course. This practice of introspection allows us to recalibrate when necessary, ensuring that our actions remain aligned with our evolving purpose. Self-reflection keeps us grounded, providing clarity and insight as we move forward.

Intention is the wind that fills our sails, guiding us through life's varied landscapes with purpose and clarity. By setting clear intentions, we steer our journey with direction, letting purpose propel us forward. This intentionality gives us the focus needed to navigate life's complexities, making each decision a step closer to our goals.

As we journey through life, our actions leave a mark on the landscape of purpose. By living with intention, we contribute to a legacy that extends beyond ourselves. Each choice we make, each step we take, shapes a path that others may follow, inspiring future generations to pursue lives of purpose and integrity. This legacy becomes a testament to the values and vision we hold dear, a lasting impact on the world around us.

Purposeful living involves walking a path that resonates with our convictions, creating a journey marked by consistency and intention. Each step we take is a testament to our dedication, leaving behind footsteps that echo with purpose. These footprints serve as a guide for others, encouraging them to find and follow their own paths of meaning and fulfillment.

The map of purpose includes monuments—markers of significant change and positive influence that endure beyond our journey. These monuments represent the meaningful contributions we make, the lives we touch, and the impact we leave behind. They serve as reminders of a life lived with purpose, standing as symbols of a legacy built on dedication, compassion, and integrity.

The map of purpose is a guide to a life of depth, intention, and fulfillment. By aligning our actions with our core values, we navigate life's challenges, embrace its opportunities, and create a legacy of meaning. This journey isn't a straight line but a dynamic, evolving path that reflects our growth, resilience, and commitment to living authentically. As we journey through life's landscapes, let purpose be the map, guiding us toward a life that is both deeply rewarding and profoundly impactful.

The Compass of Meaning

Imagine holding a map that reveals not just destinations but the values, aspirations, and milestones that make your life meaningful. This is the map of purpose—a living guide shaped by your choices, experiences, and convictions. It's not a static document but a dynamic framework that evolves as you do, ensuring every step you take aligns with a deeper sense of fulfillment.

The "MAPS" Framework for Purposeful Living

Use the MAPS framework to navigate your journey with clarity and intention:

1. **M – Mark Your Values:** Identify your core beliefs and principles. These are the landmarks guiding your decisions.
2. **A – Assess Your Actions:** Regularly evaluate whether your daily choices align with your purpose.
3. **P – Prioritize Your Path:** Focus on the pursuits and relationships that contribute to your long-term goals.
4. **S – Stay Adaptable:** Embrace change as an opportunity to refine your map, staying open to new directions and insights.

The Waypoint Strategy

To stay aligned with your purpose, use Waypoints to track progress and recalibrate:

1. **Set Clear Goals:** Define short-term and long-term milestones.
2. **Reflect on Milestones:** Celebrate achievements and learn from challenges.

3. **Revisit Your Map:** Periodically adjust your goals and strategies to reflect personal growth.

Purpose flows like a river, carving its path through the landscape of your life. At times, the current is swift, propelling you forward with clarity and energy. Other times, it meanders, inviting reflection and patience. Staying in tune with this flow allows you to harness its power and direction, ensuring your actions align with its course.

Life frequently places you at crossroads, where you must decide which path to take. These moments test your commitment to your values. Bridges, on the other hand, represent connections that help you traverse challenges or link with others who share your purpose. Together, these metaphors remind us to make deliberate choices and build strong connections.

Journaling Prompts: Charting Your Map

- What are the top three values guiding your current path? How do your daily actions reflect them?
- Recall a time when you felt deeply fulfilled. What does this experience reveal about your purpose?
- Identify one area in your life that feels out of alignment. What adjustments can you make to bring it closer to your purpose?

Visualization Exercise: The Landscape of Your Life

- Close your eyes and imagine your life as a vast, detailed map. See the mountains of accomplishment, the rivers of passion, and the valleys of challenge. Picture waypoints marking significant moments, and identify areas that feel uncharted or unclear. Envision yourself walking this map with confidence, guided by the compass of your values. What paths emerge as most meaningful?

Shift from a mindset of passivity—letting life's current carry you wherever it will—to one of deliberate action, where every choice is made with intention. Purposeful living transforms the mundane into meaningful steps along a greater journey.

Embrace the unknown territories on your map as opportunities for discovery, not obstacles to avoid. These unexplored areas hold the potential for growth, creativity, and unexpected joy, enriching your journey with new possibilities.

The Purpose Alignment Audit

Perform a monthly audit to ensure your life aligns with your purpose:

1. **Evaluate Your Time:** Are your daily activities supporting your long-term goals?
2. **Review Relationships:** Are your connections adding to your purpose or pulling you off course?
3. **Reassess Goals:** Are your aspirations still reflective of your values?

Navigating Distractions: The "Detour Discipline"

1. **Recognize Temptations:** Identify activities or habits that drain your energy without adding value.
2. **Set Boundaries:** Limit time spent on distractions, redirecting focus toward meaningful pursuits.
3. **Reward Progress:** Celebrate small victories in staying on track, reinforcing purposeful habits.

Your map of purpose is a testament to your courage, resilience, and commitment to living authentically. Each step you take reflects your dedication to a life rich in meaning and impact. Even when the path feels uncertain, trust that your values and aspirations will guide you toward fulfillment.

The most meaningful journeys are not defined by the destination but by the intention behind every step. With purpose as your compass, each choice becomes a thread in a legacy of depth, joy, and contribution.

Calibrating Your Moral Compass

Living with integrity in a world of constant noise and shifting values requires a well-calibrated moral compass. In the midst of life's chaos, integrity serves as a lighthouse, cutting through the fog of expectations and guiding us toward authenticity. Adjusting this compass isn't about adhering rigidly to rules; it's about staying aligned with what truly matters, especially when choices are complex and pressures are high.

Integrity is the North Star, the steady point of reference in a world full of distractions. By calibrating our moral compass, we set a course that isn't easily swayed by trends or temptations.

This commitment to integrity offers stability, providing a constant source of guidance as we navigate life's ever-changing circumstances. When our values are clear, our choices become clearer too, allowing us to move through life with intention and purpose.

Temptations to compromise our values can be alluring, often appearing as shortcuts or paths of least resistance. By refining our moral compass, we strengthen our ability to resist these enticing yet costly diversions. It keeps us grounded, helping us recognize and avoid decisions that might lead us away from our true path. Staying true to our values means choosing the meaningful path, even if it's not the easiest.

Life's journey is full of challenges, dilemmas, and moments that test our resolve. With a finely tuned moral compass, we have a reliable guide through this rugged terrain, helping us make choices that reflect our principles rather than external pressures. This inner guidance system allows us to stay centered in the face of difficult decisions, giving us confidence to move forward in alignment with our values.

Living with a calibrated moral compass isn't about responding to every call for action. It's about choosing purposefully, devoting our energy to what matters most. This clarity helps us focus on the people, causes, and decisions that are truly important, allowing us to give our best to what resonates with our beliefs. Purposeful choices help us create a life of depth and fulfillment, free from the distractions of trivial pursuits.

In turbulent times, authenticity serves as our ship, and integrity is its rudder. With a well-tuned moral compass, we can navigate through the storms without being thrown off course.

This steady guidance allows us to stay true to ourselves, making choices that reflect who we are and what we stand for, no matter how strong the current of outside opinions might be.

Consistency in our actions is a natural outcome of a strong moral compass. This consistency creates harmony between our values and our behaviors, reinforcing our commitment to living authentically. When our actions consistently reflect our principles, they become a powerful expression of integrity, fostering trust with others and within ourselves.

Sometimes the easiest routes lead us into uncertain territory, compromising our values for temporary gains. A well-calibrated moral compass helps us recognize these traps, keeping us aligned with the meaningful path, even when shortcuts are tempting. By choosing the path that honors our principles, we avoid the pitfalls that often come with compromise, staying true to our higher purpose.

Life often presents us with difficult choices, moments that challenge our beliefs and force us to consider what we truly value. With a well-tuned moral compass, we can face these dilemmas with clarity and grace, making decisions that honor our principles. This approach turns difficult moments into opportunities for growth, allowing us to navigate complexities without losing sight of our values.

Our moral compass acts as a lens through which our values are reflected in our actions. When calibrated thoughtfully, it ensures that our choices are aligned with our beliefs, even when under pressure. This alignment allows us to live in harmony with our values, creating a life that is consistent, intentional, and fulfilling.

Integrity is the thread that weaves our lives into a cohesive tapestry, holding together the many aspects of who we are. A finely tuned moral compass strengthens this thread, creating a life that is resilient and resistant to the chaotic forces of change. Through this careful calibration, we create a life that withstands time, challenge, and complexity, standing as a testament to the strength of our convictions.

Ethical dilemmas are often murky and complex, presenting choices that test our sense of right and wrong. A calibrated moral compass helps us navigate these quagmires, guiding us to choices that are ethically sound and true to our values. This guidance keeps us from being ensnared in compromise, ensuring that we emerge from difficult situations with our integrity intact.

Trust is the foundation of all meaningful relationships, and integrity is what nurtures that trust. By living in alignment with our values, we build trust not only in our relationships with others but also in ourselves. A finely tuned moral compass keeps our "integrity bank" rich, allowing us to foster authentic connections grounded in honesty and respect.

In moments when desires clash with values, a well-calibrated moral compass serves as an anchor. It keeps us steady, grounded in our beliefs, and resistant to choices that could lead us astray. By staying anchored in our values, we maintain a sense of stability and confidence, knowing that we're guided by principles that withstand the test of time.

Criticism is an inevitable part of life, often challenging our resolve and testing the strength of our integrity. With a clear moral compass, we can weather these storms, using criticism as an opportunity to reaffirm our values rather than sway our actions. This resilience enables us to stand firm, confident in the choices we make, even when faced with opposition.

Accountability is a dynamic process, and integrity is its guiding partner. Living with a calibrated moral compass ensures that our actions are accountable, creating a life that reflects responsibility, honesty, and commitment. This partnership fosters a sense of harmony in the choices we make, allowing us to engage with others and ourselves in a way that is respectful and grounded.

Calibrating our moral compass is more than just a set of decisions; it's a commitment to a life of integrity. Each choice becomes a step in a life well-lived, a testament to authenticity and purpose. By maintaining this compass, we navigate the chaos with clarity, conviction, and resilience, leaving behind a legacy of trust, strength, and meaningful impact.

In a world of competing values and countless distractions, a finely tuned moral compass offers the steady guidance needed to live authentically. Life's seas may be unpredictable, but with integrity as our guiding star, we chart a course toward a life rich in purpose, resilience, and meaning.

The Well-Calibrated Compass

Living with integrity is a dynamic process that requires continuous reflection and action. A well-calibrated moral compass doesn't just guide you through major ethical dilemmas; it helps you align your everyday decisions with your core values, fostering a life of authenticity, purpose, and resilience. This chapter expands the principles of a moral compass into actionable practices you can integrate into your daily life, creating a foundation for meaningful and consistent living.

1. The Foundation of Values: Unearthing Your True North

Your values are the cornerstone of your moral compass. To live authentically, you must first identify the principles that matter most to you and understand why they resonate deeply.

Practice:

Values Inventory: Set aside 30 minutes to reflect on and write down your top five core values. For each, describe why it matters to you and how it has influenced past decisions.

Alignment Check: Examine your daily routine. Are your actions consistent with these values? Identify one area where you can make a small adjustment to better reflect your core principles.

2. Navigating Temptation: Resisting Shortcuts

Shortcuts often present as easy solutions but can lead you away from your true path. Strengthening your moral compass ensures you recognize and resist these temptations.

Exercise:

Decision Map: For any tempting shortcut, write down the immediate benefits versus the potential long-term consequences. Reflect on whether it aligns with your values. Use this clarity to guide your choice.

3. Building Resilience Through Integrity

Life's challenges can test your resolve, but a strong moral compass provides the resilience to navigate tough decisions without compromising your values.

Practice:

The Integrity Anchor: During difficult decisions, pause and ask: "Does this align with the person I want to be?" Write down your response and act in a way that honors your answer.

The Accountability Mirror: End each day by reflecting on your actions. Were they aligned with your values? Acknowledge successes and identify areas for improvement.

4. Cultivating Purposeful Choices

Living with integrity involves focusing your time and energy on what truly matters, avoiding the distractions of trivial pursuits.

Exercise:

The Purpose Prioritization Matrix: Categorize tasks into "Aligned with Values" or "Distractions." Commit to reducing distractions and reallocating energy toward tasks that align with your purpose.

The One-Word Filter: Choose a single word that encapsulates your core values (e.g., "Kindness," "Honesty"). Use this word as a filter for decisions and actions throughout the day.

5. Authenticity in Action

Integrity shines brightest when your actions consistently reflect your values. Authenticity is about aligning your behavior with your beliefs, even in the face of external pressures.

Practice:

Authenticity Audit: Identify one area where you feel pressure to conform. Reflect on what changes would allow you to act in alignment with your true self. Implement one of these changes this week.

Living Your Principles: Create a personal mantra based on your values (e.g., "I act with compassion and honesty"). Repeat it daily as a reminder to align your actions with your beliefs.

6. Navigating Ethical Dilemmas

Ethical dilemmas challenge our moral compass by presenting complex choices. A clear framework helps you navigate these situations with confidence.

Framework:

4. **Identify the Conflict:** Clearly define the ethical dilemma and the values at stake.
5. **Evaluate the Options:** List possible actions and their potential consequences.
6. **Consult Your Compass:** Reflect on which option aligns most closely with your core values.
7. **Act with Integrity:** Make the choice that feels true to your principles, even if it's the harder path.

7. Strengthening the Thread of Trust

Integrity fosters trust—both with others and within yourself. Consistency in your actions builds credibility and deepens relationships.

Exercise:

Trust Journal: Write down one action each day that reinforces trust in yourself or others. Track the impact of these actions over time.

Feedback Loop: Seek feedback from trusted friends or colleagues on how your actions align with your values. Use their insights to refine your moral compass.

8. Developing Emotional Resilience

When criticism or external pressures arise, a strong moral compass provides the stability needed to stand firm in your convictions.

Practice:

The Resilience Mantra: Create a phrase that reaffirms your values under pressure (e.g., "I stay true to honesty, even when it's hard"). Use this mantra during challenging situations.

Criticism as a Guide: When faced with criticism, ask yourself: "Is this feedback aligned with my values, or is it based on external expectations?" Adjust your response accordingly.

9. The Continuous Calibration Process

Life is dynamic, and so too must be your moral compass. Regular reflection and recalibration ensure that your values remain aligned with your growth and evolving perspective.

Practice:

Seasonal Reflection: Every three months, revisit your values and evaluate whether they still reflect your current priorities and beliefs. Adjust them as needed.

The Compass Reset: When feeling lost or overwhelmed, take a day to disconnect, reflect, and realign your actions with your core values.

10. Living with Integrity: A Daily Commitment

Living with a calibrated moral compass is not about perfection but about persistence. Each day is an opportunity to make choices that reflect your highest principles and move closer to the life you envision.

Action Plan:
1. Start each day by identifying one action that aligns with your values.
2. End each day with a brief reflection on how well you lived in alignment with your integrity.
3. Celebrate small victories and commit to learning from missteps.

A well-calibrated moral compass is your lifelong guide, offering clarity and direction in a chaotic world. By integrating these practices into your daily life, you create a foundation of authenticity, trust, and purpose. Each choice becomes a testament to your integrity, shaping a life that reflects your values and inspires others to do the same.

Your moral compass isn't just a tool—it's a reflection of who you are and who you aspire to be. Keep it finely tuned, and it will lead you through life's complexities with confidence, resilience, and unwavering clarity.

Avoiding the Temptation of Drift

In the vast ocean of life, it's easy to drift—carried along by the currents of routine, external expectations, or passing trends. Living purposefully means resisting this aimless movement, choosing instead to steer intentionally toward a life of meaning and impact. When we set our sights on purpose, we chart a course through the distractions and diversions that threaten to pull us off track, creating a life defined not by chance, but by intention and depth.

Purpose is the North Star in life's sky, a constant guiding light that helps us navigate through confusion and chaos. Fixing our gaze on this guiding star ensures that our journey remains intentional, aligned with what we hold dear. When we orient ourselves around purpose, we create a sense of direction that keeps us from drifting, even when life's currents grow strong.

The temptation to settle for mediocrity can be strong, promising ease and comfort. But a life of meaning requires us to resist this pull. By aligning ourselves with purpose, we shield ourselves from the lure of complacency, striving instead for a life that reflects our true potential and values. This commitment to significance over convenience keeps us on course, preventing us from getting sidetracked by the comfort of the status quo.

Purpose acts as a powerful current, propelling us forward through life's challenges and opportunities. Embracing this current means allowing purpose to guide our actions, carrying us with intention rather than mere momentum. In this flow, we engage fully with our goals and passions, moving through life with energy and focus.

It's easy to become like driftwood, worn down by the forces of conformity and societal expectation. Avoiding the temptation of drift means choosing to live by our own values, resisting pressures that dilute our sense of self. By staying rooted in purpose, we maintain our individuality, crafting a life that reflects our true identity rather than one shaped by external influences.

Life is filled with unexplored territories, where uncertainty often tempts us to float aimlessly. But with purpose as our guide, we find the courage to navigate these unknowns with intention. Moving with purpose allows us to explore new paths with confidence, helping us chart a course that leads to growth, discovery, and fulfillment.

Living purposefully means crafting a life where each action is a note in a larger, harmonious melody. Avoiding drift means choosing our actions thoughtfully, ensuring that each one resonates with our goals and values. In this way, we create a symphony of purpose, where every decision contributes to a meaningful and coherent life.

Drift often tempts us to remain in shallow waters, where life feels predictable and safe. But true purpose requires courage—the willingness to venture into deeper, more challenging currents. By moving beyond the surface, we engage with life's complexities, discovering meaning in places that others might overlook. This journey may be turbulent, but it is also richly rewarding, bringing us closer to a life of true significance.

Aimlessness is like quicksand, pulling us down into a life without purpose. By actively choosing to pursue meaning, we equip ourselves with the tools needed to navigate life's landscapes with intention, avoiding the traps of empty routines or hollow pursuits. This focus grounds us, helping us to move through each day with clarity and purpose.

Life is filled with distractions—small, seemingly urgent matters that can pull us off track. By keeping purpose at the center of our lives, we create a beacon that cuts through the fog of daily diversions, guiding us back to what truly matters. This focus on our "why" helps us stay anchored, even as distractions try to lead us astray.

Avoiding drift isn't just about rigidly sticking to a plan; it's about creating a dance with purpose. This dance means recognizing when we're straying and making conscious adjustments to bring ourselves back on course. By aligning each step with our intentions, we move gracefully through life, avoiding the chaos of meaningless diversions and instead swaying to the rhythm of our values.

Aimless pursuits often appear as mirages—seeming to offer fulfillment but leading only to emptiness. Avoiding drift means seeing these illusions for what they are, staying committed to our true goals rather than pursuing fleeting pleasures. This discernment keeps us focused on what is real and enduring, helping us steer clear of paths that would lead us away from our purpose.

Purpose is the rudder that guides us through life's unpredictable waters. By steering with conviction, we avoid the drift that comes from indecision or doubt. This sense of direction not only moves us forward, but it also helps us navigate around obstacles, ensuring that our journey is one of progress rather than stagnation.

True purpose is fueled by intrinsic motivation—a sense of fulfillment that comes from within, rather than from external rewards. By following this inner compass, we resist the pull of superficial achievements or external validation, choosing instead to pursue goals that bring genuine satisfaction. This internal drive keeps us moving forward with resilience and dedication, no matter the obstacles.

Purposeful actions have an impact that echoes through time, leaving a lasting imprint on those we encounter. Avoiding drift means acting with this impact in mind, choosing paths that contribute positively to the world. When we act purposefully, we create ripples that inspire and uplift others, ensuring that our legacy reflects the values we hold dear.

Time is a precious resource, and purpose helps us use it wisely. Avoiding drift means being mindful of how we spend each moment, recognizing the importance of intentionality in even the smallest of choices. This awareness helps us live fully in each day, creating a life that is rich in experiences and aligned with what we truly value.

A purposeless life can feel like an endless void, an existence without direction or fulfillment. By embracing purpose, we fill this space with meaning, transforming the unknown into an adventure. This commitment to purpose gives us the courage to face uncertainty with optimism, confident in our ability to create significance from every experience.

Purpose is a steady flame, one that must be protected from the winds of distraction, doubt, and discouragement. Avoiding drift means shielding this flame, nurturing it so that it remains a constant source of light and guidance. In doing so, we ensure that our purpose continues to burn brightly, lighting the way even through life's darkest moments.

A life without purpose can feel like a bottomless abyss, an existence devoid of fulfillment. By choosing to live with intention, we steer clear of this void, creating a life filled with meaningful pursuits and personal growth. This purposeful journey fills the vastness of life with purpose, transforming what might otherwise feel empty into a vibrant tapestry of experiences.

Purpose is the wind that fills our sails, carrying us through life's ups and downs with strength and resilience. By embracing this guiding force, we chart a course toward a life that is meaningful and fulfilling. This journey may be challenging, but it is deeply rewarding, helping us to create a life that is not only well-lived but also rich in purpose and impact.

Avoiding the temptation of drift is an active choice—a commitment to live with intention, to pursue what truly matters, and to stay focused even when life pulls us in different directions. By setting purpose as our North Star, we navigate life's seas with clarity and courage, charting a course that leads us toward a life of significance, fulfillment, and lasting impact.

Anchored in Intention

Imagine being adrift in a vast ocean, the horizon stretching endlessly in all directions. Without a compass or anchor, the currents decide your path, pulling you toward destinations you never chose. Living with purpose transforms this aimless drift into a deliberate journey. Purpose becomes your compass, guiding you toward a life filled with meaning, direction, and fulfillment.

To stay intentional and grounded, use the ANCHOR framework:

1. **A – Align with Purpose:** Regularly reflect on your values and goals to ensure your actions align with your true purpose.
2. **N – Navigate Distractions:** Identify and manage the distractions that threaten to pull you off course.

3. **C – Create Intentional Habits:** Build daily routines that reinforce your purpose and keep you focused.
4. **H – Hold onto Vision:** Keep your long-term aspirations in sight, even during challenges.
5. **O – Observe Progress:** Track your achievements and recalibrate when necessary to stay aligned.
6. **R – Resist Complacency:** Push beyond comfort zones to continually grow and pursue meaningful goals.

The Drift-Defying Checklist

Each week, review this checklist to avoid slipping into aimlessness:

- Am I spending my time on what truly matters?
- Are my actions aligned with my core values and long-term goals?
- What distractions are pulling me off course, and how can I manage them?
- Have I set clear intentions for the week ahead?

Picture life as a flowing river. Without intention, you become driftwood, carried wherever the current takes you. With purpose, you become a skilled navigator, choosing the currents that lead you to meaningful destinations. Purpose transforms you from a passive passenger into an active captain of your journey.

Purpose is like a lighthouse in the stormy sea of life. Its beam cuts through the darkness of distractions and uncertainty, guiding you safely toward your true destination. By keeping your focus on this light, you avoid crashing into the rocks of aimlessness.

Journaling Prompts: Navigating with Intention

- What is one area of your life where you feel like you're drifting? What steps can you take to regain direction?
- Reflect on a time when you stayed true to your purpose despite distractions. What helped you stay on course?
- List three distractions currently pulling you off track. How can you address them to refocus on your goals?

Visualization Exercise: Setting Your Compass

- Close your eyes and imagine standing on the deck of a ship. See your destination on the horizon—a vision of your purposeful life. Feel the wind of distractions trying to steer you off course. Picture yourself adjusting the sails, using your inner compass to stay focused on your destination. With each adjustment, you feel more aligned, more intentional, and more in control of your journey.

Shift your mindset from seeing life as something that happens to you to something you actively shape. Purposeful living means becoming the captain of your ship, making deliberate choices instead of being carried along by external forces.

Life's deepest meaning often lies beneath the surface. Resist the temptation to stay in the shallow waters of comfort and distraction. By diving deeper, you discover the richness of life's complexities, finding purpose and growth where others see only challenge.

Purposeful Morning Routine

1. **Start with Reflection:** Begin each day by reviewing your intentions and aligning them with your purpose.
2. **Set Priorities:** Choose 1-3 tasks that contribute to your long-term goals.

3. Eliminate Noise: Identify potential distractions for the day and create strategies to minimize them.

Weekly "Compass Check"

- **Review Your Actions:** Reflect on whether your past week's choices supported your purpose.
- **Reaffirm Your Goals:** Revisit your long-term aspirations to ensure they remain clear.
- **Refocus Your Energy:** Identify areas where you've drifted and plan corrective actions.

Every moment you choose purpose over drift is a victory. It's a testament to your courage and commitment to living a meaningful life. Celebrate the small wins—each intentional choice brings you closer to the life you envision.

Drift is the quiet thief of meaning. By choosing purpose, you reclaim the helm of your life, steering toward horizons filled with intention, growth, and fulfillment.

Even if you find yourself adrift, remember that the power to realign is always within you. Purpose is not a destination but a practice—a continual commitment to choose direction over aimlessness.

In the vast sea of life, it's not the absence of storms that defines us, but the strength of our resolve to navigate through them with purpose.

Storms of Distractions

Distractions come in many forms, and like unpredictable storms, they can disrupt even the most carefully charted course. In the midst of life's demands, adaptability becomes our essential skill, allowing us to navigate through distractions with clarity and resilience. By embracing adaptability, we create a steady compass that helps us stay focused on our true purpose, even as the winds of distraction seek to pull us off course.

Distractions often appear when we least expect them, hidden beneath moments of calm. Recognizing that these moments may hold the seeds of future distraction prepares us to respond with intention. Adaptability allows us to face these shifts with calm and confidence, adjusting as needed while remaining rooted in our priorities.

Distractions often perform a relentless ballet, pulling us into their pirouettes of urgency and flashing lights. Adaptability is the skill that allows us to dance with these demands while staying centered in our own rhythm. By remaining in control, we can gracefully move through the day, choosing our steps and focusing our energy on what truly matters.

In today's world, digital distractions are a constant siren song, enticing us to spend endless hours scrolling, clicking, and reacting. Adaptability becomes our digital lifeboat, helping us navigate the allure of screens without losing ourselves. Setting boundaries and mindfully choosing where to place our attention enables us to stay grounded, making meaningful choices amidst the sea of notifications and alerts.

Distractions can often spiral into a whirlwind of overwhelm, leaving us feeling scattered and unproductive. Adaptability becomes our shelter, a place of stability where we can regroup and regain clarity. By creating moments of intentional pause, we can weather the chaos with resilience, maintaining focus and moving forward with purpose.

Life's distractions can crescendo into chaotic noise, each one demanding our immediate attention. Adaptability is the conductor's wand that lets us control the tempo of our day, helping us find a rhythm that aligns with our values. By choosing our own pace, we create a symphony of intentional actions rather than a cacophony of reactionary responses.

Not every distraction requires our attention. Like shooting stars, some distractions may be dazzling but ultimately fleeting. Adaptability allows us to recognize these distractions for what they are—momentary flashes that don't deserve our time. By focusing on the constellations of our goals, we can let these passing distractions fade without losing sight of our long-term journey.

Distractions can cloud our path, making it difficult to see what truly matters. Adaptability is our tool for cutting through this noise, clearing the way for focus and purpose. Whether through mindful practices, setting boundaries, or taking regular breaks, adaptability gives us the clarity needed to move forward with intention and confidence.

Some distractions have a strong pull, threatening to pull us into their orbit. Adaptability allows us to break free from these gravitational forces, giving us the ability to refocus on our goals. With adaptability as our thruster, we can avoid getting caught in the cycles of distraction and stay aligned with our greater purpose.

Life can sometimes feel like a maze filled with distractions at every turn, each one offering a different path. Adaptability is the map that guides us through this maze, helping us choose routes that align with our values and purpose. By adapting to each twist and turn, we find our way through the maze without getting lost in dead ends or aimless diversions.

In a world of constant noise, staying focused on what's essential can be challenging. Adaptability becomes our noise-canceling headset, allowing us to filter out distractions and tune in to the frequencies of focus and clarity. This skill helps us stay attuned to our priorities, blocking out the chaotic background that would otherwise compete for our attention.

Walking the tightrope of life requires balance, as distractions line each side, waiting for a misstep. Adaptability is our guide on this tightrope, helping us maintain focus and composure. By balancing carefully, we traverse this path with grace, keeping our eyes forward and our steps intentional, even as distractions try to pull us off balance.

In the cosmic canvas of life, distractions are like splashes of paint that can obscure our focus. Adaptability is our artistic brush, allowing us to blend these distractions into the background or use them intentionally to enhance the bigger picture. With this skill, we can turn distractions into part of our life's masterpiece, integrating them without letting them take over.

Each choice to adapt and refocus has a ripple effect that extends beyond the present moment. When we navigate storms of distraction with adaptability, we cultivate a mindset that strengthens our ability to remain focused over time. This focus not only shapes our present but also influences our future, helping us create a life that is rich in purpose and aligned with our truest intentions.

Avoiding the storms of distraction is an ongoing journey, one that requires flexibility, awareness, and commitment. With adaptability as our compass, we can steer through even the most chaotic waters, ensuring that our path remains clear and our focus steady. By practicing this skill, we empower ourselves to create a life defined not by distraction, but by intention, purpose, and unwavering focus.

Reclaiming Your Attention

Navigating the storms of distraction is not about eliminating distractions entirely—it's about learning to adapt, refocus, and reclaim your attention. By cultivating adaptability, you can turn these disruptions into opportunities for clarity and growth. The following actionable insights and practices offer guidance for integrating adaptability into everyday life, helping you stay aligned with your values and priorities.

1. Build Awareness: Spotting the Storms

The first step in navigating distractions is recognizing them. Often, distractions creep in unnoticed, disguised as productivity or necessary engagement.

Practice:
- **Distraction Journal:** For one week, note the distractions that pull your attention away. Write down when they occur, their source (e.g., digital, emotional, environmental), and how long they last. Use this awareness to identify patterns and triggers.

2. Establish a Daily Focus Ritual

Start your day by grounding yourself in your intentions and priorities. This helps set a clear direction and reduces susceptibility to distractions.

Practice:
- **Morning Priority Check-In:** Spend five minutes listing your top three priorities for the day. Visualize yourself successfully completing them and imagine the positive outcomes of staying focused.

3. Set Boundaries: Guarding Your Focus

Distractions thrive in unprotected spaces. Setting boundaries helps create an environment conducive to deep work and intentional living.

Practice:

- **Digital Detox Zones:** Designate specific times or spaces as "distraction-free zones." For example, keep phones out of the bedroom or set a timer to avoid endless scrolling during work hours.
- **Clear Communication:** Let others know when you need uninterrupted time, whether through status updates, physical signs (like a "Do Not Disturb" sign), or direct communication.

4. Practice Mindful Refocusing

When distractions inevitably arise, mindfulness can help you regain control without frustration or self-judgment.

Practice:

- **The Three-Breath Reset:** When you notice your attention drifting, pause and take three deep breaths. Acknowledge the distraction without judgment and gently guide your focus back to the task at hand.
- **Pause and Pivot:** Before reacting to a distraction, pause and ask yourself, "Is this important right now?" If not, pivot back to your priorities.

5. Time Management Techniques: Structuring Focus

Using structured approaches can reduce the power of distractions by providing clear timelines and intervals for deep focus and rest.

Practice:

- **The Pomodoro Technique:** Work in focused intervals (e.g., 25 minutes) followed by a 5-minute break. Use this rhythm to maintain energy and avoid burnout while staying attentive to your goals.
- **Time Blocking:** Schedule specific blocks of time for focused work, relaxation, and creative pursuits. Protect these blocks as you would a meeting or appointment.

6. Turn Digital Distractions into Allies

Rather than letting technology control your attention, use it intentionally to support your focus.

Practice:

- **Notification Management:** Disable non-essential notifications on your devices. Use "Do Not Disturb" or "Focus Mode" features during important tasks.
- **Productivity Apps:** Leverage apps like Freedom or Forest to block distracting websites or encourage uninterrupted focus.

7. Adapt to Unpredictability: Flexibility in Action

Life is unpredictable, and distractions will come. Adaptability helps you adjust without losing momentum.

Practice:

- **Reframe the Distraction:** When disrupted, ask, "How can this moment still serve my priorities?" Use interruptions as opportunities for reflection, creativity, or a quick mental reset.
- **Flexible Planning:** Build buffers into your schedule to account for unexpected distractions. This ensures minor disruptions don't derail your entire day.

8. Embrace the Power of Pause

Intentional pauses create space to reset, reflect, and refocus, preventing distractions from spiraling into overwhelm.

Practice:
- **Midday Reset Ritual:** Take a 10-minute break halfway through your day to breathe, stretch, or meditate. Use this time to assess your focus and realign with your priorities.
- **End-of-Day Reflection:** Spend five minutes reviewing what went well and what distracted you. Celebrate progress and identify areas to improve tomorrow.

9. Strengthen Emotional Resilience

Emotional distractions, like stress or frustration, can be particularly consuming. Building emotional resilience helps you manage these storms with grace.

Practice:
- **Name the Emotion:** When an emotional distraction arises, label it (e.g., "I feel anxious about this deadline"). Naming the emotion reduces its power and allows you to address it constructively.
- **Gratitude Pause:** When overwhelmed, pause to identify three things you're grateful for in the moment. Gratitude can shift your perspective and bring clarity to your focus.

10. Create a Distraction-Free Sanctuary

Your environment plays a crucial role in your ability to stay focused. A distraction-free space can serve as your refuge from the chaos.

Practice:

- **Declutter Your Workspace:** Remove non-essential items from your desk to minimize visual distractions. Keep only what you need for your current task.
- **Personalize Your Focus Zone:** Add calming elements like plants, soft lighting, or inspiring quotes to create a space that fosters concentration and positivity.

11. Learn to Let Go

Not every distraction requires your attention. Learning to let go of unimportant demands frees you to focus on what truly matters.

Practice:

- **The One-Minute Rule:** If a distraction can be resolved in under one minute (e.g., closing an unnecessary tab, responding to a quick question), handle it immediately and move on.
- **Letting Go Visualization:** When overwhelmed by distractions, close your eyes and imagine releasing them like balloons into the sky. Visualize your focus returning to your priorities.

12. Align Actions with Intentions

By consistently aligning your actions with your values and goals, distractions lose their power over you.

Practice:

- **Value-Driven Task List:** For each task, ask, "How does this align with my core values?" Use this reflection to prioritize and let go of tasks that don't serve your purpose.

- **Micro-Intentions:** Before starting any task, set a micro-intention (e.g., "I will give this email my full attention for the next five minutes"). This helps ground your focus.

The storms of distraction are inevitable, but they don't have to define your life. By integrating these practices into your daily routine, you can harness the power of adaptability to navigate through chaos with clarity and purpose. Each moment of focus strengthens your ability to weather future storms, transforming distractions into opportunities for growth and alignment.

In mastering adaptability, you reclaim control over your attention and create a life defined by intentional action, deep focus, and unwavering commitment to what truly matters. Let the storms rage; with adaptability as your compass, you'll sail through with grace, resilience, and purpose.

Rogue Waves

Life's challenges often come as rogue waves—unpredictable, powerful, and seemingly overwhelming. Resilience is the quality that transforms us from bystanders to active riders of these waves, giving us the strength to face adversity head-on. With resilience, we don't just survive the storms of life; we learn to ride them, drawing strength and skill from each encounter. This journey is not about avoiding the waves but about learning to navigate them with courage, patience, and grace.

Picture resilience as your surfboard, an instrument designed to help you master both calm and turbulent waters. It doesn't eliminate the waves; instead, it empowers you to stay balanced, even in the midst of intense challenges. By learning to trust this foundation, you gain the confidence to face whatever comes your way, knowing that resilience will keep you afloat and steady.

Resilience is about adopting a mindset that sees challenges not as setbacks, but as opportunities to showcase strength. Like a skilled surfer who embraces each wave, resilient individuals approach difficulties with curiosity and tenacity. This mindset transforms adversity into a proving ground for growth, where each challenge becomes a chance to sharpen your skills and expand your capacity.

Riding rogue waves requires balance—a skill resilience helps you develop. Whether the challenge is unexpected change, personal loss, or a daunting decision, resilience acts as a stabilizing force, helping you stay centered and prevent life's turbulence from knocking you down. Balance becomes not just a way to survive, but a way to thrive, teaching you to remain grounded regardless of the intensity of the waves.

Resilience allows you to carve your own path through life's difficulties, moving deliberately rather than passively reacting. Instead of allowing challenges to dictate your journey, you shape your course, turning each wave into an opportunity for growth. This intentional navigation helps you emerge from adversity with a deeper sense of purpose and self-direction.

When you navigate life's rogue waves with resilience, the impact goes beyond personal triumph. Your ability to face adversity with strength and optimism sends out ripples, inspiring others and contributing to a collective resilience. In this way, your resilience becomes not just a personal asset, but a gift that enriches the lives of those around you.

Hidden within each challenge are opportunities for growth and self-discovery. Resilience gives you the lens to look beyond the immediate turmoil and recognize the potential for learning and improvement. This perspective enables you to see setbacks not as losses, but as essential chapters in your journey of growth and resilience.

Resilience isn't just about weathering the storm—it's about finding ways to move with it, embracing each challenge with grace and adaptability. Like a wave dancer, you learn to respond fluidly to each situation, transforming hardship into a form of self-expression. This resilience dance allows you to engage fully with life's uncertainties, creating a rhythm that's uniquely yours.

Adversity has a way of revealing and shaping our character, allowing us to develop strengths we may not have realized we had. Resilience is the chisel that sculpts this character, helping you actively engage in the process of self-improvement. Each wave you face adds depth to your character, refining who you are and who you are becoming.

Riding rogue waves requires patience—trusting that each wave, no matter how daunting, will eventually subside. Resilience teaches you to wait for the right moment, to time your responses with intention rather than impulse. This patience is a reminder that challenges are temporary, allowing you to endure with a sense of calm and perseverance.

Life's adversities can feel like a chaotic symphony, each note unpredictable and intense. Resilience becomes your conductor's baton, allowing you to bring order to this symphony, transforming chaos into a narrative of strength. With resilience, you lead this symphony, turning dissonance into a harmonious story of personal growth and endurance.

The metaphorical "sea legs" you develop through resilience keep you steady amidst life's storms, allowing you to stand tall even when the ground beneath you shifts. This stability gives you the confidence to face future challenges, knowing that you have the strength to maintain your footing regardless of the turbulence around you.

Each wave of adversity you encounter adds to your personal evolution, transforming you into a more resilient, capable version of yourself. This journey is not about reaching a final destination, but about continuously growing through each experience. Over time, resilience becomes a commitment to personal evolution, guiding you to become a masterful rider on life's unpredictable seas.

Beyond surviving surface-level challenges, resilience allows you to dive deeper, exploring hidden aspects of your strength and potential. Like a diver exploring the ocean's depths, resilience equips you with the tools to uncover resources within yourself that might otherwise go untapped. This journey into the depths reveals insights and wisdom, helping you navigate challenges with a profound sense of understanding and self-awareness.

Life's storms often force us to look inward, reconnecting with our core values and beliefs. Resilience becomes the compass that points you back to your true north, ensuring that even in times of upheaval, you stay connected to your most authentic self. This compass keeps you aligned, guiding you through adversity with purpose and integrity.

Resilience teaches us that we have the power to shape adversity, molding our experiences into opportunities for personal development. Rather than simply enduring challenges, resilience encourages us to actively transform them, creating a narrative of strength and progress. This process turns each hardship into a meaningful contribution to our journey, one that deepens our understanding and enriches our character.

Just as the ocean is part of a larger ecosystem, so too is your resilience interconnected with the resilience of those around you. By sharing your stories of overcoming adversity, you contribute to a collective spirit of resilience, offering hope and strength to others. This shared resilience creates a community that supports and uplifts one another, fostering a sense of unity and mutual encouragement.

Resilience is about more than just surviving life's storms—it's about riding them with purpose and grace. Each wave becomes a chance to strengthen your resolve, deepen your understanding, and grow in confidence. By embracing resilience, you create a life that isn't defined by the absence of hardship, but by the ability to face each challenge with unwavering strength, transforming each rogue wave into an opportunity for growth and mastery.

Resilience invites you to gaze beyond the immediate tumult, towards the horizon of possibilities. It encourages you to dream of shores yet unseen, to envision a future shaped by your deepest aspirations. This forward-looking perspective transforms resilience from a reactive stance to a proactive journey towards realizing your full potential.

Action Plan for Time Management in the Face of Adversity

- **Prioritize Your Waves**   Just as not all waves are worth riding, not all tasks and challenges deserve your immediate attention. Prioritize based on what aligns with your values and goals.
- **Time Blocking for Surfing Sessions**   Allocate specific blocks of time to tackle challenges head-on, just as a surfer dedicates time to practice. This focused approach ensures that you're fully present for each task, turning challenges into opportunities for mastery.
- **Rest Between Sets**   In surfing, waiting for the next set of waves is as crucial as riding them. Similarly, incorporate intentional breaks between challenging tasks to recharge and reflect. This rest is vital for sustaining your resilience over the long haul.
- **Surfing in Sprints**   Approach large adversities in sprints, breaking them down into manageable sections. Tackle each part with full intensity, followed by a period of rest, mirroring the rhythm of intense surfing sessions followed by moments of calm.
- **Reflective Journaling**   After each "surfing session" or challenging period, engage in reflective journaling. This practice helps consolidate the lessons learned, deepening your understanding of resilience and preparing you for future waves.

By embracing resilience as both our surfboard and sculptor's chisel, we learn to navigate and shape the rogue waves of life with grace, courage, and purpose. This journey of resilience is not just about enduring the storm but about becoming the storm, transforming every challenge into a testament of our unyielding spirit and boundless capacity for growth.

Beyond the Known

True exploration begins at the edge of the familiar. To go beyond the known is to venture into the uncharted territories of thought, where open-mindedness is more than a virtue; it's a commitment to discovery. Life's greatest potential often lies in areas we haven't yet explored, in ideas that challenge convention and open doors to new perspectives. Embracing open-mindedness as our guide, we become pioneers in a world of possibility, discovering not just new answers, but new questions that expand the very boundaries of what we know.

Think of the mind as a vast, untamed frontier, and open-mindedness as the compass guiding you into its unexplored territories. To go beyond the known isn't about following well-worn paths; it's about blazing new trails, setting aside the safety of familiarity to explore ideas that stretch the imagination. With open-mindedness, we step into a world of potential, willing to let go of certainty in exchange for discovery.

Curiosity becomes the essential tool that cuts through the overgrowth of assumptions and conventional wisdom. When we wield curiosity with intent, we clear a path through preconceived notions, opening ourselves to new understandings and insights. Rather than avoiding the unfamiliar, curiosity invites us to lean into it, to engage deeply with ideas that defy expectation and challenge what we think we know.

Every tradition, belief, and assumption began as an idea—a lens through which people once viewed the world. Open-mindedness encourages us to revisit these "sacred" ideas, not to discard them, but to see them from new angles, allowing for growth and evolution. When we dare to question the unquestioned, we gain insights that go beyond the boundaries of established thought, transforming what we know into a more dynamic understanding.

Imagine open-mindedness as a telescope that reveals galaxies of possibility beyond the narrow scope of fixed perspectives. Instead of remaining fixed on a single point, we scan the skies of thought, instead allowing our gaze to wander, uncovering vast realms of insight and possibility. With this expanded vision, open-mindedness becomes a way of life—a willingness to explore perspectives that stretch beyond the boundaries of familiar thinking. Each new idea adds dimension to our worldview, creating a dynamic landscape of understanding that grows richer with every discovery.

Open-mindedness isn't about rejecting what's known, but about staying open to the possibility that new insights can redefine it. Just as explorers map new territories, we engage with ideas that disrupt the comfort of certainty. Breaking free from limiting patterns requires courage and flexibility, as it often means letting go of beliefs that have defined our understanding. In doing so, we cultivate the freedom to evolve, gaining a greater sense of agency in shaping the path ahead.

Just as pioneers once crossed unknown seas to discover new lands, open-mindedness allows us to sail into the unexplored waters of thought. Rather than hugging the shores of what we know, we let curiosity propel us into the deeper currents of possibility. Each new idea, each novel concept, is a compass point that redirects us, offering fresh insights and expanding our intellectual horizons. In this way, we navigate the unknown not by sticking to a fixed route, but by remaining attuned to the currents of curiosity.

When we approach knowledge with an open mind, the boundaries between "known" and "unknown" become fluid, allowing us to integrate new perspectives that may once have seemed out of reach. Open-mindedness becomes a creative force, reshaping the landscape of understanding and turning rigid mental maps into works in progress. As we venture into unfamiliar territory, we build a more complete, nuanced view of the world—one that reflects a willingness to question, adapt, and grow.

Open-mindedness requires us to seek out voices and perspectives that differ from our own, treating diversity of thought as a source of strength. When we listen to ideas that challenge us, we find new dimensions of understanding. By embracing a variety of viewpoints, we create a chorus of perspectives that enrich our understanding and help us move beyond preconceived ideas. Each voice adds a layer of depth to our knowledge, allowing us to see complex issues from multiple angles.

Every time we challenge a limitation in our thinking, we expand the map of understanding, adding new terrain to the landscape of ideas. Open-mindedness is an act of rewriting these maps, incorporating fresh discoveries and uncharted possibilities. In doing so, we break down the walls of conventional wisdom, replacing them with a world that's as dynamic and open as our willingness to explore.

Venturing beyond the known invites us to accept complexity rather than fear it. Open-mindedness helps us recognize that truth isn't always simple or straightforward; it's often multifaceted and nuanced. Embracing complexity allows us to see that knowledge isn't static but evolves as new information emerges. With an open mind, we learn to find comfort in complexity, welcoming it as a sign of growth and intellectual maturity.

When we step beyond the known, we redefine what's possible. Open-mindedness fuels this transformation, guiding us to reimagine boundaries that once felt fixed. Through this lens, each challenge becomes an opportunity to ask new questions, and every answer opens doors to further inquiry. The act of reimagining these boundaries becomes an invitation to live a life that's ever-evolving, marked by a commitment to curiosity, exploration, and growth.

Beyond the familiar lies a landscape rich with potential, a place where curiosity, open-mindedness, and resilience combine to push us forward. To go beyond the known is to embrace a mindset that welcomes each challenge, each new perspective, as a chance to deepen our understanding. With an explorer's spirit, we transform life into a journey of discovery, leaving behind the safe confines of certainty in favor of the infinite possibilities that await just beyond the horizon.

The Art of Reflection

Self-reflection invites us to step beyond the noise of daily life and confront the essence of who we are. In a world that often prioritizes speed and distraction, taking the time to reflect is a radical, deeply personal act. This journey isn't just a casual glance in the mirror; it's an expedition into the heart of our experiences, choices, and beliefs. By exploring our inner world with honesty and courage, we uncover layers of ourselves that hold the keys to growth, resilience, and authenticity.

Imagine a hall lined with mirrors that reflect every part of your life—your actions, beliefs, and choices. Self-reflection asks you to look beyond surface impressions, inviting you to witness the unfiltered, unedited version of yourself. This isn't about cultivating a flawless image; it's about seeing the beauty and complexity in your true reflection, embracing both the strengths and the imperfections that make you unique.

In a world that often pressures us to project an idealized self, self-reflection allows us to step back and appreciate the beauty of our imperfections. Each flaw, each crack in the mirror, tells a story—of resilience, growth, and transformation. By letting go of the need for perfection, we learn to value authenticity over appearances, creating space for a more genuine and compassionate self-view.

Reflection encourages us to drop the filters, to see ourselves as we truly are without the airbrushing of social expectations. This honest view includes the laugh lines, scars, and vulnerabilities that shape our journey. Embracing the raw truth of who we are is liberating, allowing us to connect with ourselves in ways that go beyond superficial approval.

Self-reflection involves engaging with all aspects of ourselves, including the parts that may be difficult to face. Shadows—the doubts, fears, and insecurities—are not to be avoided but embraced as vital parts of our inner landscape. These "shadow" elements reveal where growth is needed, offering insights that strengthen and deepen our understanding of ourselves.

Imagine your inner world as a garden in need of attention and care. Self-reflection is both the gentle nurturing and the rigorous pruning that allows growth. This process is about more than weeding out negativity; it's about cultivating resilience, self-awareness, and clarity, so that our inner garden can flourish in all its complexity and beauty.

Our emotions are the colors on the canvas of self-reflection—vibrant, sometimes turbulent, but always meaningful. Allowing ourselves to experience the full spectrum of our feelings, from joy to sorrow, anger to love, is essential to creating a true reflection of who we are. Through this emotional exploration, we create a masterpiece that reflects the depth and richness of our inner lives.

In a culture that often chases external validation, self-reflection reminds us that true approval comes from within. This inward gaze teaches us to value our own perspective, making peace with who we are rather than seeking constant affirmation from the outside. Through reflection, we develop a self-assurance that doesn't waver with external opinions, grounding ourselves in an inner source of confidence and worth.

Reflecting on our choices offers us invaluable insights. Each decision, each path taken, echoes through our lives, teaching us lessons that guide us forward. Self-reflection helps us view the past not as a series of mistakes but as a foundation for wisdom, enabling us to make more informed, intentional choices in the future.

Self-reflection is a process of removing the masks we wear, of revealing the person beneath the roles and expectations. By unmasking, we step into the truth of who we are, free from the constraints of societal pressure. This journey to authenticity is not about rejecting all we've been taught; it's about discerning which parts resonate with our true selves and embracing those with confidence.

Reflection is a journey that goes beyond surface observations, inviting us to explore the depths of our consciousness. In these depths, we discover values, desires, and beliefs that often remain hidden. By diving deeper, we gain access to insights that surface-level understanding could never reach, creating a more complete and profound sense of self-awareness.

Growth happens on the edge of comfort. Self-reflection encourages us to confront the uncomfortable truths about ourselves, knowing that it is in these moments that true transformation occurs. This willingness to engage with discomfort is a mark of courage, a step toward self-improvement that leads to resilience and personal empowerment.

Self-reflection is more than a monologue; it's a conversation with the deepest parts of ourselves. In this dialogue, we ask questions, seek answers, and confront doubts. By engaging openly with ourselves, we uncover truths that often remain hidden, fostering a relationship with ourselves that is honest, kind, and constructive.

Each insight gained through reflection becomes a thread woven into the fabric of our lives. Rather than avoiding difficult experiences, we recognize them as essential parts of our story, adding color and texture to our tapestry. Every challenge, every victory, every lesson learned contributes to a rich, nuanced portrait of who we are becoming.

Taking the time to reflect is an act of self-respect, a radical statement of self-care in a world that often promotes distraction over introspection. Through self-reflection, we give ourselves the space to grow, to learn, and to become. It's an ongoing process, a commitment to understanding and honoring the journey we're on.

As we embark on this journey of self-reflection, we reclaim the power to shape our lives, to rewrite our narratives with authenticity, courage, and compassion. In the quiet space of introspection, we find not only answers but also new questions, leading us into a fuller, more honest relationship with ourselves. This journey is one of continual discovery, an art form that deepens our understanding and enriches our lives, helping us live with intention, depth, and a profound sense of self.

The art of reflection is an expedition into the soul's wilderness, a deep dive into the waters of introspection where the pearls of wisdom are hidden. This journey isn't for the faint of heart; it requires courage to face the raw truths that lie within, to confront the shadows and the light that shape our inner landscape. But fear not, for this voyage promises the treasure of self-understanding, a prize beyond measure.

- **The Mirror of Authenticity** Cast aside the veils of pretense and peer into the mirror with honesty. It's time to engage with the person staring back at you, not with judgment, but with curiosity and compassion. This mirror reflects not just your face but the essence of your being.
- **Dialogue with the Self** Reflection is a dialogue, a sacred conversation with oneself. It's about asking the hard questions and being open to the answers, however unsettling they may be. This dialogue is the key to unlocking the chambers of self-awareness and understanding.
- **Embracing the Shadows** In the art of reflection, every shadow, every dark corner of the psyche, is an opportunity for enlightenment. These shadows are not our enemies but guides leading us to the light of deeper understanding and acceptance.

- **The Symphony of the Soul**   Just as a symphony is composed of contrasting notes and harmonies, so too is our inner world. Reflection allows us to conduct this symphony, to bring harmony to the dissonance, and to appreciate the music of our soul.
- **The Landscape of Emotions**   Our emotions are the colors with which we paint our inner landscape. Through reflection, we learn to use these colors wisely, blending joy with sorrow, anger with love, to create a masterpiece that is uniquely ours.
- **The Garden of Growth**   Self-reflection is the gardener's tool, used to prune the weeds of negativity and to nurture the blossoms of positive traits. In this garden, every thought, every feeling, is a seed that, with care, can grow into something beautiful.
- **The Path of Purpose**   Reflection illuminates the path of purpose, guiding us through the maze of life's choices. It helps us to discern which paths are worth pursuing, which are dead ends, and which lead to the fulfillment of our deepest aspirations.
- **The Forge of Resilience**   In the fire of reflection, resilience is forged. By facing our fears, our failures, and our flaws, we emerge stronger, more adaptable, and ready to face life's challenges with grace and determination.
- **The Tapestry of Connection**   Reflection reveals the threads of connection that weave us into the fabric of the universe. It shows us that we are not isolated beings but part of a greater whole, interconnected with all of existence.
- **The Horizon of Possibility**   Reflection opens our eyes to the horizon of possibility. It shows us that, no matter our past, the future is a canvas awaiting our brush, ready to be painted with the vibrant hues of our hopes, dreams, and untapped potential.

Remember that the mirror holds no judgments. It reflects, without bias, the canvas of your being. So, gaze unflinchingly, dear rebel, and let the mirror of truth be your guide in the eternal quest for self-discovery. By embracing the art of reflection, we embark on a lifelong journey of self-discovery and growth. This journey enriches not just our own lives but also the lives of those around us, as we become more authentic, compassionate, and purposeful beings. Let the hall of mirrors be your classroom, and let the lessons learned illuminate the path to your truest self.

Tools of Wisdom

Wisdom is a toolkit filled with resources for navigating life's seas, each tool designed to help us discover the treasures hidden within and around us. As we journey through the uncharted waters of personal growth and purpose, these tools serve as compasses, anchors, and beacons, guiding us toward an abundant life that's defined by meaning, connection, and self-awareness. Embracing this toolkit is about more than possessing knowledge; it's about using it with intention, curiosity, and an open heart.

Wisdom offers a compass that points not to a rigid destination but to an ever-evolving direction. With this compass, we learn to adapt to changing tides, understanding that flexibility is essential to a mindset of abundance. Each new experience becomes an opportunity to recalibrate and learn, allowing us to remain true to our values while staying open to what lies ahead.

Gratitude is the shovel that unearths life's hidden treasures. It encourages us to look beneath the surface, discovering value in the seemingly mundane and finding gems even in difficult times. Practicing gratitude opens our eyes to abundance in every experience, transforming each moment into a gift that enriches our lives.

A broad perspective helps us see abundance in all its forms, not just in material wealth. By looking through the spyglass of perspective, we broaden our view, seeing life as a rich tapestry of experiences, connections, and possibilities. This expanded vision helps us recognize that abundance is found not just in what we have, but in how we see the world.

With the telescope of vision, we look beyond the present, imagining a future filled with purpose, passion, and meaningful relationships. Envisioning our future with intention allows us to set goals that align with our values and desires, helping us shape our lives toward lasting fulfillment rather than fleeting satisfaction.

The map we follow in life is written with the ink of intentions. Rather than leaving our paths to chance, we set clear intentions that guide our actions toward meaningful destinations. When our intentions are clear, we naturally create a life abundant with purpose and aligned with our most authentic selves.

Life's winds are ever-changing, and adaptability is the sail that lets us navigate these shifts with ease. By harnessing the breeze instead of resisting it, we learn to ride the waves of uncertainty toward our goals. Adaptability becomes a key to abundance, helping us transform challenges into opportunities for growth.

Mindfulness is the anchor that grounds us in the richness of the present moment. By casting this anchor, we bring our attention to the here and now, appreciating life as it unfolds. This practice of presence nurtures a sense of abundance, reminding us that fulfillment exists in the simplicity of being.

Self-compassion opens the treasure chest of inner kindness, reminding us that true abundance begins with accepting ourselves. By embracing our imperfections, we create a foundation of self-love that enhances our ability to grow, connect, and thrive. The more we practice self-compassion, the richer our sense of worth and well-being becomes.

Self-belief is the sextant that guides us through the fog of self-doubt, helping us trust in our abilities and move forward with confidence. When we believe in ourselves, we attract opportunities and abundance, creating a life that reflects our inner strength and potential.

Resilience is the rudder that helps us stay steady through life's storms. Rather than avoiding adversity, we navigate through it with strength and resolve, understanding that challenges are temporary and that they can lead to growth. Resilience turns each hardship into a stepping stone, guiding us through the tempests toward clearer waters.

Abundance thrives in community. By surrounding ourselves with people who inspire and support us, we create a crew that helps us weather any storm and celebrate every success. Relationships are the foundation of a rich life, multiplying our joy and deepening our sense of connection and purpose.

Generosity is a lighthouse that illuminates the path not only for us but for those around us. By sharing our time, resources, and compassion, we brighten the lives of others, creating a ripple effect that returns to us in unexpected ways. Generosity reminds us that abundance grows as we give, enriching both our lives and the world around us.

The unknown often holds the keys to growth, and risk-taking is the plank we walk to reach it. By daring to step into uncertainty, we discover new perspectives, abilities, and opportunities. Risk-taking invites us to expand beyond our comfort zones, knowing that true abundance lies on the other side of calculated risks.

Wisdom includes the ability to approach life with a sense of playfulness. By letting go of seriousness, we open ourselves to creativity, laughter, and spontaneity. A playful heart draws abundance into our lives, reminding us that joy is a treasure in its own right.

Reinvention allows us to rise from the ashes of old identities, embracing transformation as a path to abundance. By letting go of outdated beliefs, we create space for new possibilities, redefining who we are with each phase of life. This ongoing renewal keeps our lives vibrant and aligned with our evolving selves.

Learning is the alchemist's elixir that transforms our understanding of the world. By staying curious and open to new ideas, we continually expand our horizons. Knowledge enriches our lives, broadening our perspectives and deepening our capacity for empathy, connection, and fulfillment.

Reflection is the compass that keeps us aligned with our values and goals. By regularly assessing our choices and actions, we make adjustments that guide us toward a more intentional and abundant life. Reflection transforms experiences into insights, allowing us to move forward with wisdom and clarity.

Possibility is the ocean upon which abundance sails. When we open ourselves to what might be, we invite a world of potential into our lives, welcoming ideas and opportunities that were previously unimaginable. Embracing possibility expands our sense of what's achievable, turning each day into an adventure of growth and discovery.

Sometimes, the most profound discoveries come from turning the telescope inward. By exploring our own potential, we uncover strengths, passions, and dreams that shape our journey. This inward gaze allows us to see ourselves as vessels of possibility, capable of creating a life filled with purpose and abundance.

Embracing the tools of wisdom equips us not only to seek abundance but to create it from within. With these tools in hand, we navigate life with intention, resilience, and joy, forging a path that's as meaningful as it is fulfilling. As we move forward, may the compass of wisdom guide us, the anchor of mindfulness ground us, and the sails of curiosity carry us toward a life rich in purpose, connection, and boundless possibility.

Where Purpose Thrives

In a world captivated by the fleeting glow of positivity, we set our sights on something more lasting: purpose. Purpose isn't a quick fix or a passing spark—it's the enduring force that shapes lives, leaving an indelible mark. This is no ordinary journey; it's a path of discovery, where meaning takes center stage and we rise above the superficial for a life that is fulfilling, dynamic, and deeply intentional.

While positivity offers moments of light, purpose gives direction. Instead of chasing after fleeting highs, we pursue a life anchored in meaning—a path that takes us beyond surface-level happiness into a realm where every choice and action carries weight. Purpose doesn't depend on ideal conditions; it weaves light and shadow into a narrative that resonates, filling life with depth and significance.

Imagine purpose as an endless odyssey rather than a brief getaway. We're not looking for a temporary escape but a journey that embraces the full scope of life. This purposeful expedition means facing both triumphs and trials, seeing every experience as a step along a path that leads to a richer understanding of ourselves and the world.

Purpose invites us to climb mountains of significance, while positivity often stays on the lower peaks of passing joy. We choose to be climbers who scale the summits of meaning, grounding ourselves in values that withstand the challenges of time. Like mountaineers tethered to conviction, we gain strength with each step upward, growing as we encounter moments that test our resolve.

Positivity may be a pleasant tune, but purpose creates a symphony—a composition that harmonizes with the many facets of our lives. Every note, every pause becomes meaningful, transforming each moment into a part of a greater whole. By weaving purpose into our lives, we create a symphony that resonates with authenticity and depth, guiding us through both quiet reflections and powerful crescendos.

Purpose is the alchemist's touch, transforming life's raw materials into something valuable. While positivity may bring a glimmer, purpose takes each experience—especially the difficult ones—and extracts the wisdom within. This process of alchemy enriches us, allowing even the mundane to become a source of growth and insight.

Rather than following well-worn paths, purpose inspires us to create our own. We are trailblazers, guided by a vision of a life that is uniquely ours. This journey calls for courage and resilience, asking us to leave behind what's comfortable in pursuit of the unknown. By forging new paths, we leave a legacy for others, showing that there is more to life than convention and safety.

Purpose is the fire that helps us walk through the coals of adversity, emerging stronger on the other side. Where positivity is a soft breeze, purpose is a powerful, unyielding force that tempers our character. Through resilience, we turn life's trials into opportunities for growth, becoming stronger with each test.

Purpose challenges the status quo, asking us to live authentically rather than conforming to expectations. We are not content with fleeting happiness or superficial contentment. Instead, we are fueled by a drive to make a difference, to live in a way that aligns with our truest selves. In this pursuit of purpose, we find the courage to live boldly, shaping our lives in alignment with what matters most.

While positivity might bring temporary warmth, purpose provides the nurturing depth that helps our lives flourish. We tend to this garden carefully, cultivating each experience so it contributes to a larger vision. This garden isn't made of instant blooms; it's a complex ecosystem of dreams, challenges, and growth that, over time, blossoms into something deeply fulfilling.

Purpose enables us to rise beyond setbacks, to move forward with renewed strength and clarity. Like a phoenix, purpose teaches us to see each challenge as part of the process, to turn every experience into a stepping stone toward resilience and understanding. Purpose is the steady flame that outlasts passing joy, providing a sense of direction and motivation that keeps us soaring.

Positivity may bring fleeting cheer, but purpose builds a lasting legacy. As we live with intention, each choice becomes a brushstroke on the canvas of our lives, creating a masterpiece that extends beyond our time. By living with purpose, we craft a legacy that inspires others, a narrative that will endure as a testament to a life well-lived.

Purpose asks us to take bold steps, to leap into the unknown with the courage to pursue what we believe in. We become explorers, guided not by comfort but by curiosity and intent. Each risk becomes a leap of faith, an adventure that brings us closer to a life filled with meaning, depth, and discovery.

While positivity might provide a momentary glow, purpose is a guiding star that lights our way. It is the map and the compass that direct our lives, pointing us toward a future that reflects our deepest values and goals. With purpose as our guide, we navigate life's seas, confident that each challenge, each joy, is part of a larger journey.

A purpose-driven life is one that chooses depth over ease, significance over simplicity. We are not chasing happiness; we are building meaning. In choosing purpose, we create a life that celebrates growth, authenticity, and impact—a life that feels both whole and fulfilling, where every step is guided by the values we hold dear.

Embrace purpose as the constant that grounds you, as the energy that drives you forward. In a world often preoccupied with quick fixes, we choose purpose as our North Star, guiding us to a life defined by authenticity, resilience, and lasting fulfillment. Let your journey be marked not by fleeting highs but by a steady, powerful commitment to a life of intent.

Cultivating the Soil of Meaning

Purpose isn't just a fleeting burst of inspiration; it's the fertile soil where the seeds of a meaningful life take root. Like a gardener tending to a diverse ecosystem, we cultivate purpose through intentional actions, resilience, and self-discovery. This chapter is an invitation to nurture the deep roots of purpose, creating a life that withstands the storms of adversity and blooms with significance over time.

The "THRIVE" Framework for Sustaining Purpose

The THRIVE framework outlines six principles for fostering a purposeful life:

1. **T – Tend to Your Values:** Identify and honor the core values that anchor your purpose.
2. **H – Harness Your Strengths:** Use your unique talents and abilities to contribute meaningfully.
3. **R – Reflect on Your Why:** Regularly revisit the reasons behind your choices to stay aligned.
4. **I – Integrate Challenges:** Embrace adversity as an opportunity for growth and wisdom.
5. **V – Visualize Your Impact:** Imagine how your actions ripple outward, influencing others and the world.

6. **E – Engage with Intention:** Be fully present in your pursuits, ensuring that each action reflects your purpose.

The Purpose Ladder

To climb toward a life where purpose thrives, think of the Purpose Ladder:

1. **Ground Level:** Identify what brings you joy and fulfillment.
2. **First Rung:** Align your daily actions with these sources of joy.
3. **Middle Rung:** Set long-term goals that reflect your values and aspirations.
4. **Top Rung:** Cultivate a legacy by contributing to something larger than yourself.

Purpose acts as both a lighthouse and an anchor—the lighthouse guiding us through uncharted waters, and the anchor keeping us steady amidst life's storms. Together, they ensure we remain on course, moving intentionally while rooted in our values.

Where positivity adds splashes of color, purpose creates a kaleidoscope of meaning. Each twist—every experience, challenge, or triumph—reveals a new pattern of insight and significance. It's this dynamic interplay of moments that forms the beauty of a purpose-driven life.

Journaling Prompts: Tending Your Garden of Purpose

- What challenges in your life have helped you grow closer to your purpose? How did they shape you?
- Reflect on a recent decision you made. How did it align (or not align) with your values and long-term vision?

- Envision a legacy you would be proud to leave behind. What steps can you take today to work toward that vision?

Visualization Exercise: Climbing the Mountain of Meaning

- Close your eyes and picture yourself at the base of a towering mountain. This mountain represents your purpose. As you climb, you encounter challenges—steep inclines, rocky paths—but also moments of breathtaking views and clarity. Visualize yourself reaching the summit, where your values and efforts converge into a sense of fulfillment. Reflect on what that summit looks like for you and the journey required to reach it.

Shift your perspective from seeking temporary happiness to building lasting meaning. While positivity can brighten a moment, purpose enriches a lifetime. This mindset invites you to prioritize depth and substance over surface-level gratification.

Recognize that purpose isn't deterred by hardship—it thrives on it. Each challenge you face becomes a stepping stone, reinforcing your resolve and deepening your connection to what truly matters.

Daily Practices to Deepen Purpose

1. **Morning Intention Setting:** Start each day by identifying one action that aligns with your long-term purpose.
2. **Evening Reflection:** End your day by reviewing how your choices contributed to your larger goals.
3. **Purposeful Connections:** Surround yourself with people who inspire and support your journey, creating a community of shared values.

Purpose Audit: Quarterly Check-In

Every three months, conduct a personal audit:

- **Assess Alignment:** Are your actions, relationships, and goals still in sync with your purpose?
- **Recalibrate Goals:** Update your objectives based on new insights or life changes.
- **Celebrate Progress:** Acknowledge milestones and the steps you've taken toward your vision.

Purpose turns the moments of your life into a harmonious symphony, where every note contributes to a larger masterpiece. Celebrate the small actions, the quiet triumphs, and the resilience you've shown in crafting a life of meaning.

A life of purpose is a life well-lived. Each choice, each step you take toward meaning, transforms the ordinary into the extraordinary, creating a legacy that will echo long after the journey is complete.

Living with purpose is not about perfection but about persistence. It's the courage to embrace uncertainty, to strive for impact, and to shape your life with intention.

Purpose is the fire that keeps you moving forward, the steady light that guides you through the darkness. In its glow, you find not only direction but also the strength to build a life of depth, beauty, and enduring significance.

Weathering Emotional Storms

Emotional storms are an inevitable part of life, often arriving with little warning but carrying a profound impact. Learning to navigate these tempests with resilience, self-awareness, and courage transforms us from passive passengers to skilled captains of our emotional journey. By embracing our feelings instead of resisting them, we can steer through life's emotional highs and lows with purpose and poise, allowing each experience to deepen our understanding of ourselves.

Imagine emotions as an internal weather system, each one a gust of wind, a flash of lightning, or a steady drizzle. Emotional resilience isn't about silencing the storm; it's about learning to dance within it. When we approach emotions as natural, necessary expressions, we create space to experience each one without judgment, allowing both the gentle breezes and powerful gales to shape our inner world.

Just as we tune into the weather, we can develop an awareness of our emotional climate. Recognizing when emotions begin to rise—whether joy, frustration, sadness, or excitement—gives us the insight needed to respond rather than react. Acknowledging emotions as they come up, like checking the forecast, helps us prepare, making it easier to manage each feeling with empathy and understanding.

Every emotion, even difficult ones, holds the potential for insight. By engaging with emotions through introspection, we transform anger into clarity, sadness into acceptance, and anxiety into awareness. This emotional alchemy allows us to draw wisdom from our experiences, helping us grow in ways that leave us better equipped to handle life's challenges.

Think of emotional resilience as the art of surfing rather than avoiding the waves. When we accept the ebbs and flows of emotion, we learn to ride each wave with grace. It's not about always finding calm waters, but about strengthening our balance, navigating highs and lows with a steady mind and heart.

Strong emotions often carry important messages. By listening closely to what each feeling is trying to tell us, we find insights that may otherwise go unnoticed. Anger may reveal an unmet need, while sadness might point to an unresolved loss. Interpreting these messages helps us develop self-awareness, allowing us to respond with greater compassion and wisdom.

Emotional regulation doesn't require us to hold back our feelings. Instead, it encourages us to release them in ways that bring relief and clarity. Allowing ourselves to feel fully—whether through journaling, speaking with a friend, or reflecting quietly—releases the weight of our emotions and renews our strength to move forward.

Each emotion contributes to the richness of our inner lives, like plants in a carefully tended garden. Embracing emotions without judgment allows us to nurture joy, acknowledge sorrow, and let all feelings find their place. This acceptance creates an inner landscape where growth is possible, even when we face challenging times.

Emotions are like the varied terrain of an internal map, complete with valleys, peaks, and uncharted territories. By exploring this landscape, we gain a deeper understanding of who we are and what we value. Knowing our emotional terrain helps us navigate more confidently, as we learn which paths to tread carefully and which hills are worth climbing.

Emotional resilience is a skill that requires practice, much like building physical endurance. By engaging in mindfulness, reflection, and self-care, we develop the strength to face intense feelings without being overwhelmed. This emotional fitness becomes a foundation, helping us weather future storms with steadiness and resolve.

Our feelings, like raw materials, can be shaped by self-awareness. Emotions such as frustration or disappointment become more manageable when we process them thoughtfully, tempering each one to create a stronger, more adaptable self. Through this process, we build an inner armor that protects without isolating, making space for both vulnerability and resilience.

Balancing emotions is a delicate act, like walking a tightrope. Emotional resilience isn't about suppressing feelings but about maintaining stability amid change. Each step is an opportunity to practice grace, navigating with a mindful awareness that embraces both stability and movement.

Our emotions are signals, guiding us toward what's meaningful, fulfilling, or necessary. By following these signals, we deepen our understanding of ourselves, using each feeling as a pointer toward our values and needs. Purpose becomes our North Star, helping us navigate emotions in ways that align with our truest intentions.

Every emotion is a thread that contributes to the rich tapestry of our lives. Embracing the diversity of our feelings allows us to weave a life that is vibrant and textured, each experience adding dimension and color. Emotional resilience is the art of integrating each thread, from joy to sorrow, into a coherent whole.

True self-awareness requires diving deep into the abyss of our emotions, exploring parts of ourselves that we may hesitate to face. Rather than skimming the surface, emotional resilience asks us to delve into the unknown, finding authenticity and strength within our innermost feelings.

Building resilience means making room for emotions rather than building walls around them. By creating open, compassionate spaces for our feelings, we allow our emotional lives to flow freely, shaping our sense of self in ways that are expansive and true.

Weathering emotional storms isn't about controlling or erasing our feelings but about learning to move with them, letting each one deepen our understanding of ourselves. By developing resilience, we gain the ability to transform emotional challenges into opportunities for growth, crafting a life that embraces every storm with strength, grace, and wisdom.

In the crucible of emotional storms, be the phoenix rising from the ashes of intensity. Emotional regulation is the alchemy of transformation, turning emotional turbulence into the fuel for rebirth. Let every emotional storm be the catalyst for your majestic rise. Success means you've not only weathered the storms but also learned to dance in the rain.

Enriching Reflections

- **Emotional Weather Journal** Keep a daily journal of your emotional weather, noting the changing patterns, storms, and calms. This practice enhances your emotional literacy, helping you to recognize and name your feelings, understand their origins, and appreciate their impact on your life.
- **Emotional Alchemy Workshop** Engage in activities that transform negative emotions into creative expression. Whether through art, writing, music, or movement, explore ways to channel your emotional energy into projects that reflect and transcend your inner experiences.
- **Garden of the Psyche Meditation** Practice regular mindfulness meditation, visualizing your emotions as plants in a garden. Contemplate their colors, textures, and what

they need to grow. This meditation encourages a nurturing attitude toward all your feelings, recognizing their value in your emotional ecosystem.

- **Compass Calibration Exercise**   Periodically assess the alignment of your emotional compass. Reflect on recent decisions and experiences to determine whether they're leading you closer to or further from your core values and life goals. Adjust your course accordingly.
- **Emotional Architecture Blueprint**   Create a visual blueprint of your emotional resilience structure. Identify the materials (strengths, coping strategies, support systems) you'll use to build it and the rooms (aspects of your life) it will contain. This exercise helps visualize and plan for a resilient emotional life.

Embrace your emotions as allies in your journey toward authenticity, resilience, and unbridled joy. Fear, joy, sorrow, love, and all other emotions are not merely reactions; they are essential ingredients for sculpting a life that is richer and more nuanced.

Your Inner Scholar

Your mind isn't a dusty archive but a vibrant center of discovery, brimming with potential for continuous learning. Engaging with new ideas, challenging established beliefs, and exploring diverse perspectives transforms your mental landscape into a dynamic haven for growth. In the pursuit of wisdom, every book, conversation, and experience becomes a source of insight, each adding richness to your understanding. Embracing continuous learning means stepping boldly into the world of knowledge with curiosity as your guide.

Learning isn't limited to the classroom; it's a lifelong pursuit that deepens with each day. Every new insight, no matter how small, builds upon the last, creating a layered, nuanced understanding of the world. To live as a lifelong learner is to approach each moment as a chance to grow, evolving with each piece of wisdom you encounter and applying it to your life in ways that enrich your experience.

Curiosity is the fuel that drives the quest for understanding. By following the "whys" that arise naturally, you open doors to new worlds of thought and possibility. Allow curiosity to lead you down paths you might not ordinarily take, for it's often on these lesser-trodden roads that the most profound discoveries await.

Diverse perspectives are the building blocks of wisdom. Engaging with ideas from various cultures, disciplines, and time periods expands your understanding and helps you see life through a broader lens. By exploring perspectives that differ from your own, you cultivate empathy and deepen your appreciation of the complex web of human thought.

Continuous learning isn't about amassing information; it's about applying knowledge in ways that matter. By using what you learn to grow in self-awareness and contribute positively to the world, you transform each insight into a tool for meaningful change. This process turns knowledge into wisdom, creating a foundation for personal and collective growth.

Consider each book, podcast, and lecture as an invitation to venture deeper into the mysteries of life. Whether diving into the sciences, exploring philosophy, or discovering the arts, each field offers unique insights that add to your personal understanding. Continuous learning gives you the chance to immerse yourself in these subjects, weaving together a rich tapestry of knowledge.

True learning requires humility—the recognition that there is always more to understand. As you grow, the vastness of what you don't know becomes even clearer. Embracing this mystery keeps your mind open and receptive, encouraging an approach to knowledge that is curious, thoughtful, and continually evolving.

An agile mind is essential in a world that's constantly changing. Continuous learning encourages flexibility, allowing you to adapt to new ideas and challenges with resilience. Each new concept or perspective challenges your assumptions, helping you develop the mental agility needed to thrive in an ever-evolving world.

Learning is a communal act, connecting you to the vast network of human thought. Each book read, each conversation had, brings you closer to the minds of those who have come before and those who walk alongside you. By participating in this exchange, you contribute to a collective wisdom that enriches not only your life but also the lives of others.

Learning is meant to be an enjoyable adventure, an exploration that brings delight as well as insight. By approaching each discovery with a sense of wonder, you turn each moment of understanding into a celebration, cultivating a love for knowledge that makes the journey itself a reward.

To live as a lifelong learner is to commit to an ongoing journey of growth and understanding. With each day, you renew your promise to seek, question, and explore the world around you.

This commitment transforms every moment into an opportunity for growth, infusing life with purpose, depth, and meaning.

Embrace the role of your inner scholar, allowing curiosity, resilience, and humility to guide you. In the world of continuous learning, there are no limits—only new horizons waiting to be discovered.

Embrace Your Inner Rebel

Unleash your inner rebel—the part of you that questions, defies, and dares to live life on its own terms. This isn't about breaking rules for the sake of chaos; it's about embodying authenticity, challenging outdated norms, and creating space for self-expression. Embracing your inner rebel means living unapologetically, with purpose and conviction, letting your life be a bold, creative masterpiece that resists conformity.

Rebels don't wait for permission to create; they forge their own paths. Instead of following someone else's guide, create your own. This path is written with conviction and marked by courage, where each choice you make adds another brushstroke to the portrait of your unique journey. To be a rebel is to live with intent, allowing purpose to shape your actions and challenge boundaries.

Let self-expression be the language of your rebellion. Whether through words, art, or style, use every aspect of your life as a canvas to communicate who you are. This isn't about fitting into society's boxes but about breaking out of them entirely, crafting a life that is as original as it is true to you.

Approval may be fleeting, but authenticity leaves a lasting impact. To live as a rebel is to prioritize integrity over popularity, staying true to yourself even when it defies expectations. This commitment to authenticity builds a legacy that resonates long after the moment has passed, leaving an imprint of courage and originality on the lives of those who encounter it.

Fear is often the barrier that keeps us from stepping into our full potential. But the rebel doesn't let fear rule; they use it as fuel. Embracing your inner rebel means turning doubts into drive, letting the energy of fear propel you forward rather than holding you back. Each step taken in the face of fear is a victory, building resilience and amplifying the voice of your inner rebel.

Labels limit, but the rebel knows they are more than a single word or phrase. Refuse to be boxed in by society's labels; instead, let your life be an evolving narrative that defies definition. As a rebel, you embrace complexity, knowing that every aspect of who you are contributes to the depth and richness of your identity.

Rebellion isn't about standing alone—it's about standing with those who share your values and vision. Surround yourself with people who inspire you, who also reject conformity and celebrate uniqueness. Together, create a community that values authenticity, innovation, and mutual support, amplifying each other's strengths and celebrating the diversity of perspectives.

Change is the constant that rebels embrace, knowing that adaptability is key to thriving in a shifting landscape. To be a rebel is to remain open to growth, to continuously evolve as you encounter new ideas and experiences. This adaptability isn't about bending to every whim but about remaining flexible and resilient, allowing you to navigate life's complexities with confidence.

True rebellion leaves a positive mark, one that echoes long after the rebel has moved on. Each choice, each action, contributes to a legacy of impact that inspires others to live boldly and authentically. To embrace your inner rebel is to create a ripple effect, influencing others to also question, create, and live in alignment with their truest selves.

Living as a rebel is not a sprint but a lifelong commitment to authenticity and courage. It's a marathon where each step forward is a statement of self-respect, a declaration of purpose, and a celebration of individuality. Embracing your inner rebel is about crafting a life that is uniquely yours, a life that challenges expectations, celebrates diversity, and leaves an indelible impact on the world.

Let the voice of your inner rebel be loud and unapologetic, a voice that speaks with integrity, courage, and passion. In a world that often seeks conformity, may your life be a reminder that true greatness lies in authenticity, and that the most profound impact comes from living with purpose and a fearless dedication to your unique path.

Liberate Your Choices

Every day, we're faced with choices that shape our lives, often influenced by a quiet yet powerful force called "Should." "Should" represents expectations—society's, family's, even our own outdated beliefs. But what if, instead of following the path of "Should," we chose the expansive road of "Could"? Embracing "Could" over "Should" is an act of liberation, a declaration of independence from obligation, and an invitation to explore life's full range of possibilities.

"Should" is fixed, a narrow set of rules imposed by habit or expectation. "Could," however, is limitless, driven by curiosity. Choosing "Could" opens doors to paths not yet considered, guided by genuine interest rather than convention. In every decision, let curiosity lead, asking not "What should I do?" but "What could I do?"

"Could" invites us to view each choice as a unique opportunity rather than a predetermined duty. In a world of "Shoulds," life becomes predictable and restrictive. But by embracing "Could," we break out of the mold and approach each day as a fresh canvas, ready to be painted in the colors of our choosing.

"Should" often leads us to make choices that align with what others expect rather than what resonates with our true selves. Choosing "Could" reconnects us to our values, desires, and dreams. By following this path, we prioritize authenticity over approval, creating a life that reflects who we genuinely are.

Imagine "Could" as a guide to living boldly and expansively. Each time you choose "Could," you take a step toward creating a life that feels intentional and unique. "Should" can feel safe but limiting, while "Could" invites you into a world of wonder and discovery. By choosing "Could," you make room for growth, exploration, and the unexpected.

"Should" is comfortable; it's familiar and unchallenging. "Could," on the other hand, often means stepping out of the comfort zone, risking failure, and embracing uncertainty. Yet, it's through these experiences that we learn, grow, and find fulfillment. Choosing "Could" is choosing growth, allowing each decision to expand who we are and what we're capable of.

"Should" often results in a life lived in grayscale—safe but predictable. "Could" brings vibrancy, adding new shades and textures to each experience. Each "Could" becomes a brushstroke on the canvas of life, contributing to a richly layered masterpiece that reflects a life fully and boldly lived.

"Should" restricts us to what's been done before, while "Could" encourages us to imagine what might be possible. By approaching life with a "Could" mindset, we transform routine moments into opportunities for creativity, innovation, and joy. "Could" is the alchemical force that turns the mundane into something remarkable.

"Should" confines us to a prescribed path, while "Could" offers wings that carry us into new territory. Every time we choose "Could," we break free from the limitations of "Should," allowing our spirit to soar. This freedom fuels resilience, helping us navigate challenges with a sense of possibility rather than restriction.

"Should" is the voice of convention, urging us to stay within the lines. "Could" is the call to adventure, encouraging us to explore beyond the boundaries and embrace the unknown. Each "Could" becomes a step on the journey toward a life filled with excitement, meaning, and depth.

A life lived in "Should" is predictable; it follows a narrow beat. But choosing "Could" creates a symphony of diverse experiences, where each decision adds a unique note to the melody of your life. This symphony celebrates spontaneity, curiosity, and the courage to live a life that is truly your own.

"Should" often defines success by external standards—what others think, expect, or approve of. "Could" invites us to redefine success on our own terms, measuring it by fulfillment, growth, and joy rather than conformity. With "Could" as our guide, we create a life that feels successful from the inside out.

Each "Could" is an invitation to live vibrantly, to paint outside the lines, and to create a life that's rich, diverse, and uniquely ours. When we choose "Could," we step into a world where each choice, each possibility, adds depth and dimension to our journey.

Embrace "Could" as a philosophy, a practice, and a daily guide. With "Could," life becomes a canvas, ready for your boldest, most authentic strokes. Break free from the constraints of "Should," and let "Could" lead you toward a life that's meaningful, joyful, and entirely yours.

The Dance of Integrity

Integrity is a dance—a dynamic, graceful movement in sync with your core values and purpose. Each step reflects authenticity, conviction, and a commitment to living a life that feels true to who you are. To dance with integrity is to live intentionally, allowing each choice, action, and interaction to align with your deepest principles. This dance is unscripted, guided by the rhythm of your unique values, and driven by a commitment to move in harmony with what matters most.

Authenticity is the rhythm that guides this dance. Living with integrity means allowing your true self to lead, moving naturally and confidently. With each step, you express who you genuinely are, free from pretense, letting authenticity shape your movements as you navigate life's challenges and joys.

Integrity allows you to choreograph a purposeful dance, each step aligned with the story you wish to tell. Rather than following a prescribed routine, you create your own, ensuring that each movement reflects a commitment to what you value. In doing so, you create a life narrative that is as intentional as it is meaningful.

Values are the dance floor upon which integrity finds its footing. Living with integrity means guarding this floor, ensuring that each step stays true to your principles. Just as a dancer moves with awareness, living in alignment with your values requires a continuous commitment to keep your path clear of compromises that don't serve your true self.

Every choice you make is a step in this dance. Living with integrity means choosing each step thoughtfully, knowing that each one contributes to the larger rhythm of your life. In the dance of integrity, there is no rush—only the deliberate movement of a life lived with purpose and care.

Integrity requires balance, a blend of conviction and adaptability. While it's essential to remain rooted in your beliefs, the dance of integrity also allows for flexibility. Moving with conviction doesn't mean rigidity; rather, it's about finding harmony between steadfastness and the willingness to adjust to life's unexpected rhythms.

Challenges are inevitable, and adversity may threaten to disrupt your dance. Integrity is about moving resiliently through these challenges, allowing obstacles to showcase your strength. Each test becomes an opportunity to reaffirm your commitment, letting your resilience shine as you navigate difficulties with grace and intention.

In the dance of integrity, accountability is essential. Living authentically means acknowledging missteps and taking responsibility when things go awry. By doing so, you keep the rhythm of your life steady and true, using each mistake as an opportunity to refine your steps and deepen your commitment.

Courage is a guiding force in the dance of integrity, leading you to face life's challenges boldly. Moving with courage means trusting yourself, stepping forward with strength even when the path is unclear. With courage as your partner, you navigate fearlessly, creating a life that reflects both intention and resilience.

Purpose infuses each movement with joy and significance. By dancing with integrity, you allow purpose to shape each step, celebrating the alignment between your actions and your deepest values. This joyful dance becomes a testament to a life lived meaningfully, bringing fulfillment to every step.

Your dance of integrity leaves a legacy. Each choice, each interaction, and each expression of authenticity contributes to a life that inspires others. By dancing your own dance with conviction, you encourage others to embrace their own unique paths, leaving a legacy that resonates with honesty, courage, and purpose.

The dance of integrity is an unscripted, lifelong performance, a celebration of values, authenticity, and purpose. It is not about perfection but about movement that reflects the true rhythm of who you are. In a world that often pressures us to follow the steps of others, let your dance be a courageous, authentic expression of a life aligned with what truly matters.

The Jar of Careful Choices

Welcome to a mindful approach to emotional investment, a concept that reframes the way you allocate your emotional energy. Picture a jar that collects your moments of genuine care and concern, each one representing a unit of your emotional capital. Let's call it the "Jar of Careful Choices"—a place where you consciously decide which concerns, people, and causes are worth investing in. This Jar helps you practice intentionality, making sure your emotional investments yield returns in fulfillment, growth, and joy rather than stress or depletion.

Think of your care and attention as valuable currency. The Jar of Careful Choices prompts you to ask where and why you spend this currency, ensuring each investment reflects your values and priorities. When you guard your resources thoughtfully, every emotional investment becomes more impactful and fulfilling.

Not every concern or situation deserves your investment. The Jar teaches you to reserve your energy for what truly matters, ensuring that your emotional resources aren't wasted on trivial or unworthy distractions. In doing so, you make room for experiences and relationships that align with your values.

If you spread your emotional energy too thin, it loses its impact, much like a currency in oversupply. The Jar of Careful Choices encourages you to keep your investments purposeful, reserving your energy for moments and people who bring real meaning to your life. This way, your emotional capital retains its value and importance.

Just as a strong financial portfolio is diversified, a balanced emotional life involves investing in different areas—relationships, hobbies, personal goals, and community involvement. By spreading your emotional resources, you build resilience and a richer, more balanced life that can weather the ups and downs.

Life will require you to make "withdrawals" of emotional energy in times of crisis or when loved ones need support. When you manage your resources wisely, these withdrawals feel purposeful and rewarding, leaving you with a sense of fulfillment instead of depletion.

Relying on external validation to replenish your emotional reserves can create dependency. Instead, the Jar of Careful Choices encourages you to build a robust internal reserve, focusing on self-care and personal boundaries so you can navigate emotional challenges independently and with strength.

When you invest emotional energy wisely, you receive dividends in the form of meaningful connections, personal growth, and shared joy. These returns make every thoughtful investment worthwhile, reinforcing your sense of purpose and emotional wealth.

Impulsive emotional reactions may feel satisfying in the moment but often lack lasting value. The Jar reminds you to pause and consider where your energy is truly needed, encouraging thoughtful responses that lead to greater emotional well-being.

Some investments are worth taking, while others are best avoided. The Jar teaches you to hedge your bets, choosing when to fully invest and when to hold back. By protecting your emotional energy, you're better prepared to handle unexpected challenges with resilience.

Each investment you make shapes the legacy you leave behind. The Jar of Careful Choices is about building an emotional legacy of purpose, kindness, and authenticity. Through intentional decisions, you contribute to a legacy of meaning and impact for yourself and those around you.

Ultimately, emotional wealth isn't about how much energy you give but the quality of each investment. By practicing intentionality and valuing your resources, the Jar of Careful Choices guides you toward a life rich in meaningful experiences and genuine connections. May every investment bring you closer to a life filled with purpose, joy, and resilience.

Your Most Potent Sorcery

Enter the transformative world of passion-fueled goal setting—a practice that turns ordinary ambitions into extraordinary achievements. Imagine this process as a kind of alchemy, where you channel your deepest passions into meaningful goals, infusing each one with the clarity, courage, and commitment necessary to bring them to life. This alchemy isn't just about reaching a destination; it's about creating a journey rich with purpose, resilience, and self-discovery.

Passion is the spark that ignites your goals, transforming vague ideas into powerful aspirations. In this alchemy, clarity is essential. Begin by refining your goals until they resonate with your values and purpose, stripping away what's unnecessary to reveal the core of what truly matters. Clear, purpose-driven goals become the foundation upon which passion can work its transformative magic.

Passion acts as the elixir that keeps you motivated, even when challenges arise. As you pursue your goals, resilience becomes the crucible that tests your commitment. Each setback becomes a learning opportunity, an essential part of the alchemical process that strengthens your resolve. Passion, fueled by resilience, keeps you moving forward, no matter how challenging the journey may be.

Harness the power of the MAGIC framework to transform your goals into meaningful achievements:

1. **M – Map Your Vision:** Clearly define what you want to achieve and why it matters.
2. **A – Align with Values:** Ensure your goals reflect your core beliefs and passions.
3. **G – Generate Momentum:** Break goals into smaller, actionable steps to maintain progress.
4. **I – Ignite Resilience:** Embrace challenges as opportunities to grow stronger and more determined.
5. **C – Celebrate Milestones:** Recognize progress to fuel motivation and reinforce your commitment.

The practice of setting MAGIC goals brings structure to your aspirations. Each goal becomes an intentional step in the alchemical journey, shaped by clear intentions and fueled by passion. MAGIC goals ensure that your efforts are not just aimed at achieving something, but at creating a life filled with purpose and meaning.

Fear is often a weight that holds us back. But in the alchemy of passion, fear is transformed into courage, becoming the catalyst that propels you toward growth. By facing fear, you refine it, converting it into a resource that drives you to take bold steps. This process teaches you to see challenges not as obstacles but as essential elements in the transformation of your life.

Life rarely follows a straight path, and goals are no different. Adaptability allows you to remain committed to your vision while staying open to adjustments along the way. As the landscape of your life changes, let flexibility be a core part of your process, embracing the unexpected as an integral component of the journey. This adaptability keeps your goals fresh and aligned with the evolving direction of your life.

Visualization is a powerful tool in the alchemy of passion. By vividly imagining your goals as already achieved, you create a mental roadmap that guides your actions. Visualization is not just dreaming—it's a focused, intentional practice that solidifies your commitment, making each step toward your goals feel more achievable and grounded in reality.

Reflection is essential to any journey of growth, allowing you to assess progress and adjust as needed. Regularly taking time to reflect on your path ensures that each step aligns with your evolving vision. This process of reinvention turns each goal achieved into a stepping stone for new beginnings, creating a continuous cycle of growth and exploration.

Acknowledging each milestone fuels motivation and reinforces your commitment. Celebration doesn't need to be grand; it's the act of recognizing progress that matters. Each step toward your goal is a moment to reflect on your growth, honoring the journey and encouraging you to keep moving forward with renewed energy.

True alchemy transforms not only the self but also the world around you. As you work toward your goals, consider how your journey can positively impact others. When your goals serve a greater purpose, your passion becomes a source of inspiration and empowerment, enriching not only your life but the lives of those around you.

When you approach your goals with passion, adaptability, and resilience, you create a legacy of purpose and fulfillment. Each goal you set and achieve becomes part of a greater story, one that reflects your dedication to living a life filled with meaning. This legacy is a testament to the power of passion-driven goals—a reminder that, through intentional effort, you can transform your life into a masterpiece.

Let the alchemy of passion be your guide, transforming each goal into a meaningful milestone. With clarity, resilience, and a vision that reaches beyond the ordinary, may your journey become a testament to what's possible when you infuse life with purpose and an unwavering commitment to growth.

Journey into the heart of where passion meets purpose, and transform the raw materials of your aspirations into the gold of realized dreams. This is a spellbook for the courageous, ready to harness their deepest desires and channel them into the creation of a life that echoes with the vibrancy of true fulfillment.

1. **The Cauldron of Clarity**   Begin with absolute clarity. Like the alchemist seeking the philosopher's stone, your journey requires a clear vision. Distill your desires to their purest form, ensuring that your goals are not just reflections of fleeting wishes but beacons guiding you towards your authentic self.

2. **The Elixir of Motivation**   Let passion be the elixir that sustains you. When the path becomes difficult, and shadows lengthen, sip from this potion to renew your spirit. Passion is not just fuel; it's the very essence of your journey, imbuing your actions with meaning and your goals with the possibility of achievement.

3. **MAGIC Goals as Alchemical Equations**   Employ MAGIC goals as your formula for transformation. This framework is your spell for turning leaden aspirations into golden outcomes, ensuring that each goal is a step towards the extraordinary.

4. **The Philosopher's Stone of Courage**   Use courage to transmute fear. In the alchemical process of pursuing your passions, fear often emerges as the base metal. With courage, however, you possess the philosopher's stone capable of turning this fear into the gold of opportunity and growth.

5. **The Laboratory of Life**   Embrace life as your alchemical laboratory. Experimentation is the essence of discovery. Mix, try, fail, and refine. Each attempt, each failure, is a precious ingredient in the potion of success, leading you closer to the masterpiece you seek to create.

6. **The Crucible of Resilience**   Let resilience be your crucible, within which the true strength of your goals is tested and forged. Face the flames of adversity with the knowledge that what emerges will be stronger, more beautiful, and infinitely more precious.

7. **The Sorcery of Focus**   Harness the sorcery of focus, directing your energies with laser precision. In the realm of goal achievement, distraction is the enemy. Focus your powers on what truly matters, allowing your passions to guide you through the fog of the inconsequential.

8. **The Mystic Art of Visualization**   Visualization is your mystic art, the practice of seeing the unseen, of bringing

the future into the present through the power of your mind's eye. Visualize not just the goals but the steps, the challenges, and the triumphs. Let this vision be the map that guides you through the uncharted territories of your ambitions.

9. **The Dance of Adaptability**   Master the dance of adaptability. Goals, like the alchemist's elements, can change states. Fluidity is not a sign of weakness but of wisdom, allowing you to navigate the ever-changing landscape of life with agility and grace.

10. **The Goldsmith's Workshop of Achievement**   View each goal as a piece in the goldsmith's workshop. Here, raw ambitions are carefully shaped, refined, and polished until they shine with the luster of achievement. This meticulous process turns goals from mere intentions into tangible successes.

11. **The Alchemist's Hourglass**   Time is your alchemist's hourglass, reminding you that each moment is a finite resource to be utilized with intention. Manage this resource wisely, allocating your moments to pursuits that will shape the masterpiece of your life.

12. **The Symphony of Dreams**   Let your goals compose the symphony of your life, a harmony of dreams that sings with purpose and passion. Each goal, each achievement, is a note in this melody, contributing to the opus that is your legacy.

Embrace this journey not as a mere pursuit of goals but as an alchemical transformation. Let the passion that fuels your desires be the fire that transmutes your dreams into reality, crafting from the ordinary an existence that resonates with the extraordinary. In this sorcery, find not just the achievement of goals but the unveiling of your true masterpiece: a life lived with purpose, passion, and profound fulfillment.

The Spellbook of Transformation

In our ancient spellbook, every incantation represents a goal infused with your unique passions and dreams. This is the essence of passion-fueled goal setting—your most potent sorcery. It's a magical process of turning the raw materials of ambition, resilience, and vision into a life of extraordinary achievement and meaning.

The Alchemical Process: Turning Passion into Gold

1. **The Base Metal (Idea):** Start with raw ambitions. Write down everything you want to achieve, no matter how big or small.
2. **The Refining Fire (Clarity):** Strip away superficial desires, focusing on what truly resonates with your purpose.
3. **The Crucible (Resilience):** Face challenges head-on, knowing they are necessary for transformation.
4. **The Philosopher's Stone (Adaptability):** Adjust your approach without losing sight of your vision.
5. **The Gold (Fulfillment):** Achieve your goals and reflect on how they contribute to your life's greater narrative.

Think of your goals as ingredients in a cauldron. Passion is the flame beneath it, turning disparate elements into a cohesive and powerful elixir. Each step you take—every plan, adjustment, and effort—stirs the pot, bringing your vision to life.

Your goals are like arrows, and passion is the force that propels them. Without clarity (aim) and resilience (steady hands), your arrows may miss the target. By focusing on your purpose, you ensure each shot is deliberate, powerful, and meaningful.

Journaling Prompts: Casting Your Spells

- What are three goals that ignite your deepest passion? Why do they matter to you?
- Reflect on a past goal you achieved. What challenges did you face, and how did overcoming them shape you?
- Visualize a current goal as already achieved. How does it feel, and what steps will you take next to make it a reality?

Visualization Exercise: The Alchemist's Laboratory

- Close your eyes and imagine a laboratory filled with tools of transformation. See your goal as raw material, like unpolished metal. Picture yourself refining it—removing distractions, adding passion, and applying effort. Watch as it transforms into something brilliant and valuable. How does this process inspire your next step?

Reframe challenges as necessary components of the alchemical process. Just as fire tempers steel, difficulties strengthen your resolve and refine your character, making your achievements more meaningful.

Understand that even the most powerful spells are composed of small, intentional actions. Each deliberate step contributes to the transformation, proving that greatness lies in consistency and persistence.

Daily Rituals for Goal-Setting Sorcery

1. **Morning Intention Spell:** Begin each day by setting one specific, passion-aligned goal to focus on.
2. **Midday Momentum Check:** Review your progress and adjust your approach as needed.

3. **Evening Gratitude Ritual:** Reflect on what you achieved, no matter how small, and acknowledge its significance in your larger journey.

The Adaptive Spell: Flexibility in Goal Setting
1. **Recognize Shifts:** Monitor when external circumstances or personal growth require changes to your goals.
2. **Reframe Failures:** View setbacks as experiments that provide valuable insights.
3. **Reignite Passion:** Regularly revisit why your goals matter to keep your motivation alive.

Every step you take toward your goal is a spell cast toward transformation. Celebrate these moments, knowing that they contribute to the larger masterpiece of your life.

True sorcery lies in your ability to transform dreams into reality, step by step, fueled by passion and guided by purpose.

The goals you achieve don't just impact you—they inspire others, leaving a legacy of courage and determination. Your journey becomes a beacon, showing others what's possible when you embrace your most potent sorcery.

Your life is an alchemical masterpiece, crafted from the fire of your passion and the resilience of your spirit. Let each goal be a testament to the magic you carry within.

The Comfort Zone

The Comfort Zone is a place that feels cozy, familiar, and safe, yet it's also a space where growth stagnates and dreams dim. True transformation requires stepping beyond its soft, familiar boundaries into the exhilarating unknown. Embracing the discomfort that comes with change is where authentic growth happens, where resilience is built, and where life takes on new depth and meaning. By stepping out of the Comfort Zone, you allow yourself to explore, evolve, and discover your true potential.

While the Comfort Zone provides a sense of security, it can also stifle ambition and creativity. Choosing to move beyond comfort is a declaration that growth is more important than convenience. Discomfort may feel unfamiliar, but it is a powerful catalyst, pushing you to expand, adapt, and transform in ways you never imagined possible.

The Comfort Zone offers a sense of stability, but often this safety is an illusion that limits your potential. While stepping outside may seem risky, it is actually the path to greater resilience and strength. By challenging the familiar, you learn that real security comes from adaptability and courage, not from staying within prescribed limits.

Routine and predictability can lull you into complacency, but life's true fulfillment lies beyond what's known and comfortable. Breaking away from the ordinary opens doors to new experiences, relationships, and insights. Each venture into unfamiliar territory brings you closer to a fuller, more vibrant life, where every step forward is an accomplishment.

The Comfort Zone might shield you from immediate struggles, but it also prevents you from developing resilience. True strength is forged in the face of challenges, and stepping into discomfort allows you to build the skills necessary to navigate life's inevitable ups and downs. Each setback becomes a stepping stone, shaping a mindset that sees adversity as an opportunity for growth.

Comfort often brings a sense of routine, but purpose thrives in exploration and challenge. When you step beyond the familiar, you open yourself to discovering passions and pursuits that may otherwise have remained hidden. This willingness to explore deepens your connection to a life driven by intention rather than habit.

Fear of failure often keeps us rooted in comfort, yet failure is one of life's greatest teachers. By embracing potential setbacks, you learn resilience, humility, and the confidence that comes from knowing you can rise again. Failures become badges of experience, reminders that you dared to try, learn, and grow.

Life outside the Comfort Zone is an adventure that enriches you with new perspectives and experiences. By choosing to leave the familiar, you embark on a journey that expands your understanding of the world and your place within it. Embracing the unknown isn't about abandoning safety but about choosing a life of discovery and self-awareness.

Each step beyond the Comfort Zone contributes to a legacy of courage and resilience. When you prioritize growth over comfort, you set a powerful example for others, demonstrating that life's fullest experiences are often found outside the boundaries of the familiar. This legacy is one of strength, inspiration, and transformation.

Make the choice to leave the comfort of the familiar behind. Step boldly into the unknown, where each challenge is an opportunity for growth and each experience adds richness to the journey of becoming who you are meant to be. Embrace the adventure of growth, and let it be the sculptor that shapes you into your most authentic, resilient self.

The Canvas Isn't Infinite

Time is like a blank canvas, but it's a finite one—every brushstroke, every choice, shapes your life's artwork. Time management is the art of sculpting meaning and purpose into each day, balancing the practical with the profound, the planned with the spontaneous. Here, every moment counts, and the key lies in being intentional about where your energy goes.

Every day is an opportunity to sculpt a masterpiece with the hours at your disposal. Choose your activities with intention, understanding that focus is the foundation of meaningful time management. Distractions may be tempting, but each moment spent on what truly matters transforms your day into a powerful work of art.

Multitasking is often a tempting shortcut, but it's more sleight of hand than true productivity. While it seems efficient, multitasking actually splinters focus and robs you of depth. Embrace the power of single-tasking instead, giving each task the attention it deserves, and watch as your accomplishments gain clarity and quality.

A to-do list is not a catch-all but a tool for prioritization. Simplify your list by identifying tasks that genuinely contribute to your goals and aspirations. By focusing on what is most meaningful, you prevent your list from overwhelming your time and attention, leaving you empowered rather than burdened.

Procrastination can feel like a mountain, but with discipline, you can climb it. Embrace small steps to start, breaking tasks into manageable actions. Each moment you commit to overcoming procrastination moves you closer to your goals, turning obstacles into opportunities for growth.

Think of time blocking as curating your day, placing dedicated timeframes around specific tasks to ensure they get done. By compartmentalizing work, relaxation, and personal growth, you create balance, allowing yourself to be fully present in each activity.

Routines are the gears that keep your life moving forward. A well-constructed routine brings structure without rigidity, providing a foundation that frees your mind to focus on what truly matters. Embrace routines as supportive allies, helping you create consistency and momentum.

Rest is not a break from productivity; it's a part of it. A well-rested mind is creative, resilient, and capable of handling challenges. Honor rest as an integral part of time management, understanding that a refreshed mind is more productive, focused, and able to create its best work.

Think of your calendar as a map, guiding you through a balanced blend of responsibilities and enjoyment. Schedule time for your priorities, but also leave room for moments of joy, spontaneity, and exploration. A well-designed calendar isn't a restriction; it's an invitation to live fully.

Carve out time for self-reflection. Reviewing your week's achievements, setbacks, and lessons learned allows you to adjust and refine. Reflection provides insight into how you can manage your time better, aligning your days more closely with your goals and values.

Learning to say "no" protects your time from unnecessary distractions. By turning down commitments that don't serve your priorities, you create space for what genuinely matters. Saying "no" is an empowering choice that strengthens your dedication to living intentionally.

Your approach to time management shapes not only your present but also the legacy you leave behind. Each choice, each hour spent thoughtfully, becomes part of a larger story—a timeless piece of who you are. Craft your days with purpose, allowing each to build upon the last, creating a life that reflects a legacy of intentional living.

Time is finite, but with purpose and intention, you can transform each moment into something extraordinary. By choosing wisely, celebrating small victories, and honoring rest, you shape a life that's as fulfilling as it is impactful. Each day is a brushstroke on your canvas; let every one of them count.

Let the echoes of efficient chiseling, intentional carving, and the occasional rebellious stroke linger in the air. Carry the masterpiece of your time sculpture with pride, for it's a testament to your ability to craft a life that reflects your priorities. Onward, skilled sculptors of time to the action plan for mastering time management where you select strategies that genuinely resonate with you and your unique path in life.

Action Plan and Activities for Mastering Time Management

- **Daily Canvas Evaluation** Each morning, visualize your day as a blank canvas. Decide on three main "brushstrokes" (tasks) that will most significantly contribute to your masterpiece (goals). Sketch these out in your planner or a dedicated app.
- **Multitasking Myth-Busting Challenge** For one week, consciously avoid multitasking. Tackle tasks sequentially, noting any differences in productivity and the quality of work.
- **Taming the To-Do List Beast** Transform your to-do list into a prioritized action plan. Divide tasks into "Must Do," "Should Do," and "Could Do" categories. Focus on completing the "Must Do" tasks first to prevent your list from becoming overwhelming.
- **Time Blocking Garden** Schedule your week using the time blocking method. Assign specific tasks to dedicated blocks

of time, including blocks for breaks and leisure. This helps create a balanced "garden" of productivity and relaxation.

- **Routine Reinforcement**   Establish a morning routine that kickstarts your day on a positive note. Include elements such as meditation, exercise, or reading. Note how this impacts your mood and productivity throughout the day.
- **Buffet-Style Time Management Reflection**   At the end of each day, reflect on how you "filled your plate" with activities. Were you selective, or did you overindulge in time-wasting activities? Plan adjustments for the next day.
- **Deadline Symphony**   For each project or task with a deadline, create a mini-symphony. Break down the project into movements (phases) and set mini-deadlines for each. This helps maintain a rhythmic progression toward your final goal.
- **Urgent-Important Matrix Dojo**   Apply the Urgent-Important Matrix to your tasks weekly by drawing lines that divide a piece of paper into quadrants. Label Quadrant 1: Urgent and Important (Do First), Quadrant 2: Important but not Urgent (Schedule), Quadrant 3: Urgent but Not Important (Delegate) and Quadrant 4: Not Urgent and Not Important (Eliminate). Sort tasks into the matrix's quadrants and tackle them according to their categorization. Reflect on how this clarifies your priorities and enhances decision-making.
- **Mindful Minute Resets**   Incorporate regular "mindful minutes" into your day. Use these moments to breathe deeply, center yourself, and realign with your goals. Observe how this practice affects your focus and stress levels.
- **Identify and Banish Time Vampires**   Keep a log of activities for a week. Identify "time vampires" that drain productivity. Develop strategies to minimize or eliminate these from your schedule.

- **Rest Renaissance** Schedule regular rest periods and activities that rejuvenate you. Acknowledge these as crucial for sustaining long-term productivity.
- **Quantum Leap Prioritization** Periodically reassess your priorities. Visualize them as elements in a quantum field, flexible and adaptable. Adjust your focus and actions to align with any shifts in priorities.
- **The Art of Saying "No"** Practice saying no to new commitments that don't align with your priorities. Reflect on the empowerment this brings and its impact on your time management.
- **Celebration of Small Wins** At the end of each day, jot down small victories. Acknowledge how these contribute to your larger goals and enhance your motivation.
- **Calendar Cartography** Treat your calendar as a map of your personal journey. Ensure it reflects a balance of tasks, personal time, and unplanned adventures.
- **Reflective Time Sculpting:** Dedicate time each week to reflect on your time management practices. Adjust your strategies and techniques based on insights gained from these reflections.
- **Rule Breaking** Once a month, deliberately break away from your structured time management plan. Engage in spontaneous or creative activities, noting the impact on your creativity and overall well-being.
- **Legacy Time Management Reflection** Consider how the way you manage your time contributes to the legacy you're building. Align your time management practices with the legacy you wish to leave behind.

Painting with Intention

Imagine your life as a vast but finite canvas, where each moment is a brushstroke shaping the masterpiece of your existence. The colors you choose, the precision of your strokes, and the care you take determine the depth and vibrancy of the final image. Time, though limited, offers infinite possibilities for meaning when approached with purpose and artistry.

Master your time with the ART framework:

1. **A – Assess Your Priorities:** Regularly evaluate what truly matters to you. Which activities align with your values and goals?
2. **R – Refine Your Focus:** Eliminate distractions and concentrate deeply on one task at a time.
3. **T – Transform Time into Meaning:** View every moment as an opportunity to create something valuable, whether it's progress, connection, or rest.

The Brushstroke Method

To manage time effectively, treat each day like a brushstroke in your life's painting:

1. **Outline the Vision:** Start with clarity—what's the big picture you're aiming for?
2. **Choose Your Palette:** Select tasks that add value to your life, ensuring a balance of work, relationships, and personal growth.
3. **Layer with Care:** Prioritize quality over quantity, allowing each task to build meaningfully on the last.

Time management is like sculpting—each decision carves away what's unnecessary, revealing the masterpiece within. Just as a sculptor works with care and precision, you shape your life by focusing on what truly matters, removing distractions that detract from your vision.

Think of your day as a symphony, with each task representing a note. Distractions create discord, while intentional focus brings harmony. By composing your time thoughtfully, you create a melody of productivity and fulfillment that resonates deeply.

Journaling Prompts: Designing Your Day

- What activities bring the most meaning to your life? Are you allocating enough time to them?
- Reflect on the past week. What tasks felt most fulfilling, and which ones drained your energy unnecessarily?
- Imagine your day as a canvas. What would you like to see painted on it by the time the day ends?

Visualization Exercise: Crafting the Canvas

- Close your eyes and picture your day as a blank canvas. See yourself adding brushstrokes for meaningful activities, bold colors for moments of joy, and soft tones for rest. Imagine stepping back at the end of the day to admire the balance and intention in your creation. How does this inspire your choices today?

Shift your mindset from equating busyness with productivity to recognizing that depth and focus define true accomplishment. By valuing quality over quantity, you create a life where each moment contributes to a larger purpose.

Instead of lamenting the finiteness of time, see it as a gift that compels intentionality. The canvas's edges remind us to make each stroke count, turning limitations into opportunities for meaningful expression.

The Time Artist's Daily Ritual

1. Morning Intention Setting: Begin the day by identifying your top three priorities.
2. Midday Check-In: Review your progress and adjust if distractions have crept in.
3. Evening Reflection: Celebrate what you've achieved and refine your approach for the next day.

Time Blocking for Masterpieces

1. Divide and Conquer: Allocate specific blocks of time for tasks that require focus, rest, and spontaneity.
2. Guard Your Gold Hours: Protect the time of day when you're most productive for your most important work.
3. Balance the Palette: Ensure your schedule includes not just responsibilities but also joy, creativity, and rest.

Each day, no matter how ordinary, holds the potential for extraordinary meaning. Celebrate the small victories—whether it's completing a task, sharing a meaningful conversation, or taking a moment to rest. These moments are the brushstrokes that create a life of purpose.

Your canvas may be finite, but its impact can be infinite. Paint boldly, live intentionally, and create a masterpiece that reflects your truest self.

By managing your time with care and purpose, you leave behind a legacy that inspires others. Your choices become a testament to living fully, reminding others to approach their own canvas with creativity and intention.

Each moment is a brushstroke. With purpose and passion, you can transform the canvas of your life into a work of art that inspires and endures.

The Procrastination Dragon

The Procrastination Dragon is a familiar foe to anyone who's ever delayed a goal or put off a task. It's a master of disguise, cloaking itself in the promise of "tomorrow" and hiding behind excuses, distractions, and the illusion of perfection. Facing this dragon isn't just a battle against laziness; it's a deeper confrontation with the fears and doubts that keep us from taking action. But don't fear, for you're equipped with tools and insights to not only face this dragon but to tame it.

Procrastination often stems from deeper fears: fear of failure, fear of success, and even fear of the unknown. These fears thrive in the shadow of perfectionism, making the smallest step seem monumental. The dragon's whispers of "later" feed off these fears, creating a cycle of delay that, over time, saps your energy and motivation. Recognizing these underlying emotions is the first step to breaking free from procrastination's grip.

Procrastination finds a home in the comfort zone—a place where nothing ever risks failure or rejection. While comfort may feel safe, it's also where dreams and goals can fade into inaction. Embrace the idea that progress isn't about perfection; it's about movement. The comfort zone may feel secure, but true growth comes when you're willing to step beyond it and try, even if the outcome isn't flawless.

The Procrastination Dragon thrives on the illusion that time is endless. It lures you into believing that tomorrow will be the perfect time to start. Yet, as each day passes, the mountain of tasks grows taller. The key to overcoming this is action, no matter how small. A single step, however minor, disrupts the cycle of "later" and brings your goals into the present moment.

Procrastination feasts on overwhelm, making tasks seem insurmountable. When you break down big goals into smaller, manageable steps, you can take action without feeling burdened. By tackling one piece at a time, you reduce the power of procrastination and gain momentum toward meaningful progress.

Busywork often gives the illusion of productivity, but it shields procrastination by focusing on tasks that don't truly move you forward. Identify what really matters and prioritize tasks that align with your goals. By cutting through busywork, you weaken procrastination's defenses and focus on actions that create real results.

Distractions—whether social media, emails, or minor tasks—are like sirens calling you away from your path. Set boundaries with these distractions by blocking specific times for focused work. When you guard your attention, you reclaim control and make space for meaningful progress.

Procrastination often feeds off self-doubt, convincing you that you're not ready or capable. Replace self-doubt with self-compassion by acknowledging your strengths and valuing progress over perfection. Every step forward, no matter how small, reinforces your ability to succeed.

The Triple Sprint Method is a powerful approach to reclaiming productivity. Break your tasks into three focused, timed sprints—each around 20–30 minutes. After each sprint, take a brief break. This method reduces overwhelm, keeps you engaged, and transforms even the most daunting tasks into manageable challenges.

"Tomorrow" is a tempting promise, but each time you choose "now" over "later," you reclaim power over procrastination. Begin by choosing one small task you've been delaying and commit to completing it today. When you build a habit of taking immediate action, you create a foundation of momentum that carries you forward.

Procrastination guards one of life's greatest tragedies: the unlived potential. Every dream delayed, every goal postponed, adds to a life less fully lived. But when you confront procrastination, you liberate your potential and create a legacy of intentional choices and realized ambitions. Each action you take contributes to a life well-lived, a life marked by courage, growth, and fulfillment.

Procrastination may be a fierce dragon, but armed with awareness, discipline, and a commitment to act now, you can reclaim your time, your dreams, and your purpose. Begin the rebellion against procrastination by embracing the power of the present moment and allowing each step to bring you closer to the life you envision.

Ultimately, facing procrastination is a dance with the dragon— a dance where you lead. It's a dance of courage, of stepping into the arena despite the fear, and of moving to the rhythm of your purpose and passion. This battle isn't just about time management; it's about soul management. It's about conquering the fears, doubts, and illusions that feed the dragon and reclaiming the kingdom of your potential. The time to act is now. The place to start is here. The person to do it is you. Let's dance, for today, we arm you with a powerful weapon: The Triple Sprint Method. This isn't just a strategy; it's your battle plan for reclaiming your kingdom of productivity from the clutches of procrastination.

1. **Identifying the Beast.** Your first step in this epic quest is to identify the task you've been avoiding—the dragon lurking in the shadows of your to-do list. It's that one task that seems so daunting, you'd rather face an actual dragon than tackle it. But here's the twist: break down this monstrous task into smaller, more manageable dragons. These mini-beasts won't seem nearly as intimidating.

2. **The Art of the Triple Sprint.** Armed with your segmented task, initiate the Triple Sprint. Set a timer for 20 minutes, and dive into battle against the first segment

of your task. During this sprint, all distractions must be banished to the realm of "Not Now." Your focus is your sword, cutting through excuses and delays.

3. **The Sacred Pause.** After your first 20-minute sprint, the bell tolls for a sacred pause. This isn't a retreat; it's a strategic regrouping. Take deep breaths, stretch your limbs, and refresh your surroundings. This brief respite is the magical elixir that rejuvenates your spirit for the next charge.

4. **Charging Forward.** Reset your timer and plunge back into the fray, attacking the next segment of your task or continuing your assault on the first if the beast is stubborn. With each 20-minute cycle, you're not just working; you're weaving a spell of productivity, turning daunting tasks into achievable victories.

5. **The Reward of Rest.** After three cycles of relentless pursuit (totaling 60 minutes of focused effort), grant yourself the boon of a 15-minute break. This is your time to wander the castle grounds, feast, or simply bask in the glory of your efforts. This is essential to replenish your energy for the battles ahead.

6. **The Cycle of Momentum.** Continue the rhythm of 20-minute focused work intervals followed by 15-minute rejuvenating breaks, diligently progressing through the steps of your task until its completion. Each cycle is a balanced blend of concentrated effort and meaningful relaxation, designed to optimize both productivity and well-being.

7. **Reflection in Victory.** With each task conquered, take a moment to stand atop the mountain of your achievement and reflect. How did the Triple Sprint Method serve you in battle? Were the dragons of distraction kept at bay? Did the rhythm of focus and rest invigorate your spirit?

8. **Adjusting Your Armor.** No warrior remains clad in the same armor for all battles. Reflect on the pacing of your sprints, the effectiveness of your breaks, and the overall strategy. Adjust your approach as needed, for the Procrastination Dragon is cunning and ever-changing in its tactics.

Let the Triple Sprint become your rhythm in the dance of productivity. With each task approached in this manner, you're not just doing work; you're performing a ritual that celebrates focus, discipline, and well-being. The journey doesn't end with one task. The Procrastination Dragon has many heads, and your quest is ongoing. But fear not, for you now possess a powerful strategy that transforms overwhelming battles into series of victorious sprints. In the end, what you're fighting for is time—precious, irreplaceable time. The Triple Sprint Method doesn't just help you win battles; it helps you reclaim your time, allowing you to spend it on the pursuits that truly matter in the grand saga of your life.

Awakening the Dragon

Procrastination is no ordinary foe—it is a cunning and persistent dragon that guards the gates of your potential. Its power lies in its ability to disguise fear as comfort and delay as rationality. But within you lies a hero armed with clarity, courage, and actionable strategies. The battle isn't about defeating the dragon once but learning to confront it every time it rears its head. Let's prepare for the quest.

The "DRAGON" Framework for Overcoming Procrastination

Use the DRAGON framework to confront and tame procrastination effectively:

1. **D – Define the Beast:** Identify the specific task or fear fueling your delay.
2. **R – Reframe Your Perspective:** View the task as an opportunity for growth, not a burden.
3. **A – Act in Small Steps:** Break down tasks into manageable actions that feel achievable.
4. **G – Guard Against Distractions:** Create a distraction-free environment to focus fully.
5. **O – Own Your Wins:** Celebrate small victories to build momentum and confidence.
6. **N – Navigate Setbacks Gracefully:** Treat failures as part of the process, not as reasons to stop.

Picture yourself as a knight standing before the Procrastination Dragon. The dragon's fiery breath represents your fears—fear of failure, imperfection, or the unknown. Your sword is a single, intentional action. Each strike doesn't slay the dragon but weakens its hold, empowering you to take the next step in your quest.

Procrastination is like a mountain that grows taller the longer you wait to climb it. With each delay, the peak seems more distant, and the climb more intimidating. But every small step upward chips away at its height, proving that progress, not perfection, is the key to reaching the summit.

Journaling Prompts: Taming the Dragon

- What tasks or goals have you been avoiding? What fears or doubts might be fueling your procrastination?
- Recall a time when you overcame procrastination. What strategies or mindsets helped you succeed?
- Write down one small action you can take today to begin confronting a task you've been delaying.

Visualization Exercise: Facing the Dragon

- Close your eyes and imagine standing before the Procrastination Dragon. Its scales shimmer with excuses, its breath carries the heat of doubt. Picture yourself wielding a sword made of focus and courage. See yourself taking one bold step toward it, cutting through the excuses with a single action. Feel the dragon retreat as you advance, growing stronger with each step forward.

Transform your fear of starting into curiosity about what lies on the other side of action. Ask yourself: "What might I discover or achieve if I take the first step today?" Viewing tasks as experiments rather than tests reduces the pressure to be perfect and encourages progress.

Procrastination thrives on the illusion of "later." Commit to the mantra: "Now is better than perfect." By taking action in the present, you gain momentum, shifting from stagnation to flow.

The Ritual of Focus

1. **Prepare Your Battleground:** Remove distractions—put your phone on silent, clear your workspace, and set an intention for the task at hand.
2. **Set the Timer:** Start with a short, focused burst of work (15–20 minutes) to overcome the initial inertia.

3. **Reflect and Reset:** After completing the burst, take a brief moment to evaluate your progress and plan the next step.

The Fear-to-Action Strategy
1. **Acknowledge the Fear:** Write down what's holding you back (e.g., fear of failure).
2. **Counter with Action:** Identify the smallest possible step to counteract the fear (e.g., write the first sentence of a report).
3. **Celebrate the Win:** Acknowledge that taking even a small step is a victory over procrastination.

Every time you face the Procrastination Dragon, you reclaim not just your time but your power. Celebrate the small victories—each task completed, each fear overcome. These are the building blocks of a life lived with intention and purpose.

The Procrastination Dragon is fierce, but it cannot withstand the steady force of action. Each step forward, no matter how small, is a triumph over fear and delay.

When you conquer procrastination, you build a legacy of intentionality and growth. Your actions inspire others to face their own dragons, proving that courage and commitment are the keys to a life of fulfillment.

Time is the most precious treasure we have. By choosing to act today, you honor its value and create a masterpiece from the moments you've been given.

Purpose is Not a Unicorn: The Real Quest for Meaning

Purpose isn't a mythical creature dancing in the realm of unattainable dreams. It's not something you stumble upon in a self-help book or add to your online profile for show. Purpose is the heartbeat of your life—the intentional pursuit of what truly matters, of what stirs your spirit and shapes your actions. In essence, purpose is about giving intentional care and attention to the things that bring meaning to your existence.

Purpose isn't a decorative phrase or a status symbol. It's the steady foundation that keeps you grounded through life's storms. It's the drive that makes you rise in the morning and keeps you anchored when everything else is in flux. Purpose goes beyond the surface, infusing your life with resilience and direction. When times get hard, it's the core commitment that holds you steady.

Purposeful living involves choosing pursuits that resonate deeply, that add meaning to your journey. Instead of scattering energy across countless endeavors, focus on those that genuinely matter to you—the people, causes, and ideas that make your heart beat faster. That's the essence of a life lived with intentionality.

Think of purpose as your North Star—not a distant, unreachable dream, but a constant presence that guides you, providing clarity amid life's uncertainties. When the path ahead is foggy or filled with challenges, purpose illuminates the way, helping you navigate with confidence and direction.

Purposeful living isn't about simply existing. It's a symphony of passions and values, harmonizing to create a life that feels vibrant and fulfilled. Whether it's through creativity, work, relationships, or service, allow your passion to take center stage, enriching each moment and leaving a lasting impact.

Imagine your time and energy as valuable resources. Purposeful living means investing these in ways that bring genuine satisfaction and alignment. Rather than scattering your efforts, direct them toward what adds depth to your life, making each action a purposeful investment in your own growth and joy.

Purpose isn't a distant goal; it's an active, daily commitment. Live it in each interaction, each choice, and each challenge you face. Let it propel you forward, adding joy to your day and meaning to your nights. Purpose is a dynamic, evolving force that grows as you do, adapting to life's changes while always guiding you forward.

In a world that often values conformity, purposeful living is an act of quiet rebellion. It's about choosing to walk your unique path, even when it diverges from the expected route. It's a way of saying, "I'm here to live a life true to myself," not just fit a prewritten mold.

Part of purposeful living is recognizing when certain paths no longer align with who you're becoming. It's okay to release pursuits that no longer serve you. Embracing change with purpose means letting go of what doesn't resonate and making space for new, meaningful possibilities.

Purpose extends beyond personal fulfillment; it has a ripple effect. Living with purpose inspires those around you, creating a legacy that goes beyond your immediate circle. When your life is guided by purpose, it becomes a light for others, encouraging them to seek meaning and fulfillment as well.

Imagine each action as a stone tossed into the lake of life, creating ripples that extend beyond yourself. Purposeful living considers this ripple effect, understanding that each choice and action has the potential to inspire, uplift, and contribute positively to the broader world.

Purposeful living is about aligning your actions, relationships, and choices with the principles that matter most. This alignment transforms life into a cohesive and satisfying journey, where each day builds on the last, leading toward a greater sense of fulfillment and harmony.

Challenges aren't roadblocks; they're part of the purposeful journey. Each obstacle becomes an opportunity for growth, adding depth and resilience to your pursuit of meaning. Embrace challenges as integral parts of your purpose, building your capacity to navigate life's complexities with wisdom and strength.

Cultivate relationships that enrich your journey, connecting with others who share or support your sense of purpose. Periodically reflect on your progress, celebrating successes and learning from setbacks. Purpose is strengthened by these reflective pauses, recalibrating your path to ensure you're moving forward with clarity.

Purpose isn't confined to your life alone; it's part of the legacy you leave. Every choice, action, and relationship becomes part of the lasting impact you make. Think of purpose as your contribution to the world—a meaningful footprint that endures beyond your lifetime.

Gratitude adds richness to purposeful living. It's about appreciating each opportunity, challenge, and relationship that shapes your journey. By acknowledging the gifts in each moment, you deepen your connection to your purpose, reinforcing the value of the path you've chosen.

Your life is a masterpiece in progress, painted with the strokes of intention, passion, and resilience. Purpose is the guiding hand, shaping this work of art into something uniquely yours—a testament to a life well-lived, true to your values, and impactful for others.

Let purpose be your guide, a dynamic and evolving source of direction that transforms each day into a meaningful adventure. Live fully, authentically, and with a commitment to what matters most, and you'll find that purpose isn't something you chase; it's something you create.

The Real Magic of Purpose

Purpose isn't a mythical unicorn galloping just out of reach. It's a steady and grounding force—a practical, living presence that guides your actions and shapes your life. Purpose is found not in rare, dazzling moments but in the quiet, consistent choices that align your life with your values. The quest for meaning isn't about finding something elusive; it's about creating something enduring.

The "BEACON" Framework for Living Purposefully

Use the BEACON framework to guide your pursuit of purpose:

1. **B – Begin with Values:** Identify your core beliefs and principles. Purpose starts with knowing what matters most to you.
2. **E – Evaluate Your Actions:** Regularly assess whether your daily choices align with your values and goals.
3. **A – Adapt as You Grow:** Allow your purpose to evolve as your experiences and understanding deepen.
4. **C – Cultivate Meaningful Connections:** Surround yourself with people who inspire and support your journey.

5. **O – Observe the Ripple Effect:** Recognize how your actions impact others and contribute to the greater good.
6. **N – Nourish with Gratitude:** Celebrate the small wins and appreciate the journey, reinforcing your commitment to purpose.

The Purpose Pyramid

Visualize your purpose as a pyramid with three foundational layers:

1. **Foundation (Values):** The base of your pyramid is built on your core principles and beliefs.
2. **Structure (Goals and Passions):** These are the pursuits and activities that align with your values, giving your purpose a tangible shape.
3. **Summit (Legacy):** At the top is the lasting impact you wish to leave—a testament to the life you've lived and the contributions you've made.

Purpose isn't a single destination; it's the compass that points you in the right direction, even when the path is unclear. Life's storms may shift your course, but with purpose as your guide, you'll always find your way back to what truly matters.

Think of your purpose as a lighthouse. It not only guides your own journey but also illuminates the way for others, helping them navigate their own paths to meaning. Every action you take is a beacon that inspires and uplifts those around you.

Journaling Prompts: Unveiling Your Purpose

- What activities or moments make you feel most alive and fulfilled? How can you incorporate more of these into your life?

- Reflect on a time when you felt deeply connected to your purpose. What circumstances or choices led to that feeling?
- Write about the legacy you want to leave. How do your daily actions contribute to this vision?

Visualization Exercise: Building Your Purposeful Path

- Close your eyes and imagine a winding path stretching out before you. Along the way are milestones—moments of alignment, growth, and contribution. Picture yourself walking this path, each step guided by your values and passions. Visualize how the journey evolves, leading you to a life of meaning and fulfillment.

Stop chasing purpose as if it's something outside of you. Instead, focus on creating it through intentional choices and actions. Purpose isn't something you find; it's something you build, piece by piece, through the way you live your life.

Purpose is not a rigid ideal but a dynamic force that evolves with you. Embrace the adaptability of purpose, knowing that it can expand, shift, and deepen as you grow and face new experiences.

Daily Purpose Ritual

1. **Morning Intention Setting:** Begin each day by identifying one action that aligns with your values.
2. **Midday Alignment Check:** Pause during the day to reflect on whether your actions are serving your purpose. Adjust as needed.
3. **Evening Gratitude Reflection:** End your day by celebrating one meaningful action you took and acknowledging its contribution to your larger journey.

The Legacy Ladder
1. **Step 1: Identify Your Core Values:** Write down three to five principles that define your life.
2. **Step 2: Set Purposeful Goals:** Align your short-term and long-term goals with these values.
3. **Step 3: Take Consistent Action:** Break your goals into manageable steps and commit to daily progress.
4. **Step 4: Reflect and Refine:** Regularly review your progress and recalibrate as needed to stay aligned.

Every step you take toward purposeful living is a victory. Celebrate the small actions, the quiet moments of alignment, and the ways you've stayed true to yourself. Purpose is not a single achievement but a lifetime of meaningful choices.

Purpose is not a unicorn; it's the steady, grounding force that shapes your life. It's in the steps you take every day, the values you hold, and the legacy you leave behind.

Your pursuit of purpose doesn't just impact you—it creates a ripple effect that inspires and uplifts others. By living authentically and intentionally, you show the world what's possible when life is guided by meaning.

The real quest for meaning isn't about chasing the extraordinary; it's about finding the extraordinary in the everyday. Live with purpose, and let your life be a testament to what truly matters.

March Headlong into the Chaos

Strap on your inner armor, grab the shield of adaptability, and step into the arena of life with the confidence to face its unpredictable turns. Life showers us with challenges like confetti at a parade—it's time to master the ancient art of "triage," knowing when to handle the paper cuts and when to focus on the deeper, more meaningful needs.

Imagine life as a grand stage of unpredictable acts, where you're the lead dodging curveballs and navigating plot twists. Adaptability is your backstage pass, letting you flow through each act without losing your balance, transforming obstacles into scenes of growth.

Think of life as an emergency room where you're both doctor and patient. Adaptability becomes your toolkit, giving you the skills to triage each problem, from minor distractions to the truly urgent, with discernment and grace.

Every adaptable soul needs a Triage Toolkit: humor to take the edge off, resilience to keep going, and perspective to see beyond the immediate challenge. These tools are honed not by theories but by experience, forming the foundation of a life led with courage and creativity.

Consider adaptability like a mental agility drill; it's your response to life's unexpected jolts—a broken shoelace, an offbeat meeting, or a disrupted plan. It's the calm and resourcefulness that allows you to solve life's "small problems" without letting them become emotional landslides.

Adaptability also equips you with the perspective to assess what really matters. Some priorities are like rubber balls—able to bounce back if dropped—while others are as fragile as glass. The skill lies in knowing which to let go and which to handle with care.

Adaptability is not about eliminating chaos; it's about finding balance in the midst of it. Picture a Zen master poised amidst a whirlwind—that's the adaptability Zen, staying calm not because the chaos stops but because you've learned to surf the currents.

Adaptability allows you to face uncertainty like a ringmaster in life's circus. Instead of fearing the chaos, you flow with it, knowing that each twist can be met with resilience and flexibility. After all, it's the moments when plans fall apart that we uncover new ways forward.

Balancing adaptability means dancing along the tightrope of life's challenges, spreading your arms wide and embracing the wobble. It's learning that balance isn't about rigid control but about the graceful sway that keeps you centered amid change.

Adaptability is like a dance—a rhythm that moves with life's unexpected beats, allowing you to twirl through adversity with intention. It's not about rehearsing every step but learning to adjust, to let the beat guide you, and to stay centered through life's improvisational turns.

In a world that leans toward control, adaptability is a quiet rebellion. It's about thriving in the unknown, creating meaning in places where others might only see disruption. It's the courageous decision to make your own path through shifting sands.

Adaptability is also the art of surrender—not as a defeat but as wisdom. It's discerning when a challenge is worth your energy and when it's best to let go, trusting that resilience will see you through in ways even planning cannot.

Adaptability means dancing in the rain, finding beauty in the unpredictability of each day. It's the ability to pace yourself through the storm, knowing when to pause, when to press forward, and when to let life unfold as it will. In this way, adaptability becomes the thread that connects all challenges into a cohesive, vibrant life story.

Let adaptability be your anthem—a song of courage, a rhythm of resilience, a melody of embracing life's many forms. Raise your shield of adaptability high, knowing that life's challenges are opportunities, and that every twist is a chance to grow in strength, wisdom, and joy. The world is your arena, and you are the warrior dancing with the beautiful chaos of existence.

The Busyness Epidemic

Take a step back, breathe, and reclaim the rhythm of your own life. The busyness epidemic has captured us in its relentless cycle, convincing us that constant activity equals purpose. It's time to dismantle this myth and redefine what it truly means to live meaningfully and with intention.

Busyness has become an unexamined idol. Let's demystify it: constant frenzy doesn't make us productive; it makes us disconnected. We've become a society that worships the rush, but true fulfillment lies in learning to slow down and savor.

Wearing busyness like a badge of honor? Tear it off. Exhaustion is not a status symbol, nor is it a testament to success. The real mark of achievement is balance—a pace that fuels rather than drains us.

Striving to "win" in the Busyness Olympics only leads to burnout. Opting out isn't failure; it's freedom. Our worth isn't measured by our to-do lists but by the depth and sincerity we bring to each experience.

If downtime feels like a guilty indulgence, it's time for a reset. Downtime is not laziness; it's the pause that gives life its harmony. Embracing quiet moments allows for true connection—with ourselves and with what we genuinely care about.

A calendar that's crammed to the edges? Trim it down. True rebels see their schedules not as checklists but as spaces for intentional action. Leave room for spontaneous moments, for the unexpected joys that can only appear in unplanned spaces.

Saying "yes" to everything is unsustainable. Master the art of saying "no" without regret, honoring your time as the rare resource it is. Spend it on pursuits that align with who you truly are and where you want to go.

The allure of multitasking is an illusion of productivity that only fractures our focus. Instead, practice the art of presence, investing fully in each task and trusting that quality of attention will yield far greater results than divided energy.

Sometimes, it's wise to choose to miss out. FOMO isn't just social; it's also about a relentless pursuit of "doing" as though more means better. Rebels understand the power of meaningful idleness, of letting go of the need to be constantly engaged.

Burnout isn't a badge; it's a warning sign. Pace yourself, recognizing that the journey isn't won in sprints but in sustainable steps. To move with purpose is to recognize that rest is not an interruption of life but an essential component of it.

Productivity isn't about volume; it's about alignment. A handful of purposeful actions create more impact than a dozen rushed tasks done without heart. Rebels value quality, choosing depth over breadth.

Digital chaos only adds to the frenzy. Make room for tech-free moments where you can reconnect with the analog world, where you can relish simplicity and rediscover what it means to be fully present.

In the race against time, the richness of life can blur. Slow down to notice the beauty in ordinary things—the moments that fill our days and the simple pleasures that bring quiet joy.

Rest is the radical act that fuels resilience. Prioritize sleep, not as a reward but as a right. When we're rested, we find clarity, creativity, and the strength to resist the gravitational pull of the busyness epidemic.

By shedding the busyness mindset, we open ourselves to a life lived intentionally, where meaning thrives in presence, not in perpetual motion. This is where our legacy takes shape—not in the noise of constant activity, but in the profound simplicity of being fully engaged in each moment.

The busyness epidemic has entrenched itself in the very fabric of modern existence, heralding a false dawn of productivity that often leads to burnout rather than genuine achievement.

In this relentless pursuit of doing more, we've unwittingly surrendered the reins of our lives to a ceaseless cycle of tasks, meetings, and notifications, each clamoring for our dwindling attention. This epidemic, however, is not an invincible foe; it's a construct of our collective making, and just as we have built it, so too can we dismantle it. The journey towards reclaiming our time and essence begins with a conscious decision to prioritize depth over breadth, meaning over mere activity.

1. **Prioritize Depth Over Breadth** Embrace the art of doing less but better. This means making the tough choices about what truly deserves your time and energy. It's about digging deeper into fewer pursuits that resonate with your core values rather than skimming the surface of many.

2. **Cultivate Mindfulness and Presence** In a world that glorifies busyness, the act of being fully present becomes a radical form of resistance. Mindfulness practices not only counteract the scatterbrain syndrome induced by chronic busyness but also enhance our capacity to engage deeply with the task or moment at hand.

3. **Establish Boundaries** The busyness epidemic thrives in the absence of clear boundaries. By setting firm limits on work hours, technology use, and even the types of engagements we commit to, we can create a sanctuary for focus, creativity, and rest.

4. **Embrace the Art of Slow Living** Slow living is not about doing everything at a snail's pace; it's about doing things at the right pace. This means allowing ourselves the time to immerse fully in activities, to savor experiences, and to perform tasks with care and attention.

5. **Redefine Productivity** Productivity should not be measured by the quantity of tasks completed but by the significance of our contributions. This shift in perspective

encourages us to focus on impact rather than activity, on creating lasting value rather than ticking off to-do lists.

Action Plan for Tackling the Busyness Epidemic:

- **Daily Mindfulness Practice**   Dedicate at least 10 minutes each day to mindfulness or meditation to cultivate presence.
- **Weekly Priority Review**   At the start of each week, identify your top three priorities that align with your values and goals. Focus your energy on these areas.
- **Technology Time-Outs:** Implement regular technology breaks throughout your day. Consider "tech-free" evenings or weekends to disconnect and recharge.
- **Slow Living Rituals**   Incorporate rituals into your routine that encourage slow living—this could be a leisurely walk, cooking a meal from scratch, or practicing a craft.
- **Reflection and Journaling**   End your day with a reflection session. Use journaling to contemplate the day's activities, what you learned, and how you felt. This practice fosters mindfulness and helps you stay aligned with your core values.

By adopting these strategies and embracing the principles laid out, you can begin to carve out a life marked not by busyness but by meaningful engagement and purposeful living. Challenge the prevailing winds of the busyness epidemic and chart a course towards a more intentional, fulfilled existence.

In the rebellion against busyness, you'll discover the profound art of living authentically, unburdened by the chains of perpetual motion. The rebel's path is one of intentional action, not mindless reaction. It's time to reclaim your time, your sanity, and your essence. Turn the page; the rebellion begins now.

The Theatre of Judgement

Step into the spotlight. In the theater of judgment, the critics have claimed the best seats in the house, armed with sharp opinions and ready to cast their reviews. But remember, this show isn't a tragedy; it's your life—a story as intricate as it is untamed. Let's explore this grand spectacle where your authenticity takes center stage and judgment merely fills the seats.

The critics are eager, dissecting your every move like characters in a play. But here's the thing: their reviews do not define your script. They might have a front-row view, but they don't hold the pen.

Master the dramatic pause. Let your critics hang in suspense, and savor the power of keeping them guessing. They may expect a specific storyline, but your life's plot is yours to twist and reveal.

Let authenticity be your standing ovation. The world craves originality, yet judgment often censors it. Step onto the stage with the kind of truth that leaves even the harshest critics in awe.

Critics love to monologue, dissecting choices and narrating flaws, but remember, their voices fade when your self-belief stands unshaken. Listen to their soliloquy, and then steal the scene with your own unapologetic confidence.

In this theater, reject the trap of perfection. Critics revel in perfection's illusion; instead, embrace your imperfections—they are the strokes that make your story one-of-a-kind. Let your bold performance silence the noise of judgment.

The real magic happens backstage. Take moments away from the spotlight to recalibrate, to fine-tune your values, and to shed the weight of others' expectations. Every encore you deliver will be all the more powerful when it's aligned with who you are.

Your self-worth isn't decided by applause or criticism. Some will cheer, some will jeer; but walk your own path, a path where your value isn't swayed by others' judgments.

Remember, the harshest critics are often grappling with their own insecurities, projecting their fears onto the stage of your life. Stand firm in your story, knowing that the weight of their words says more about them than it does about you.

When the curtain falls, your performance—a bold, unapologetic masterpiece—transcends the fleeting opinions of the audience. Take a bow, virtuoso. You've crafted a story that defies judgment, one that echoes long after the critics' voices fade. This theater may be judgmental, but you, my friend, are the architect, the artist, and the fearless lead in a life well-lived.

The Photoshop Rebellion

It's time to smash the glossy facades of superficiality and celebrate the beautifully unpolished, unapologetic truth of who we are. This isn't a beauty contest; it's a full-scale rebellion, a defiant stand against perfectionism and pretenses, calling us all to drop the filters and embrace the chaotic artistry of authenticity.

Imagine the world as a masquerade ball, where everyone wears masks of curated perfection. Superficiality revels in this charade, an illusion that seeks to define us by what we show on the surface. But we're not here to dance in disguise; we're here to tear off the masks and revel in our true, raw selves.

Superficiality is the airbrush rebellion, where imperfections are edited away to create an illusion. But life isn't a retouched image; it's a rich tapestry woven with mistakes, lessons, and stories that make us who we are. We're here to embrace the authentic beauty that emerges when we refuse to smooth out the rough edges.

In this world, it's as if we've all become mannequins, striking rigid, lifeless poses to fit society's mold. But we are not statues; we're here to break free from the contrived postures and step into the spontaneity of life. Let's shatter the illusion of flawlessness and move to the rhythm of authenticity.

Superficiality operates like an illusionist, creating a spectacle of appearances that distracts from what's real. But we're done applauding the magic tricks. We're stepping onto the stage to share our unfiltered stories, letting authenticity light up the room.

In a culture obsessed with beauty myths, superficiality tries to rewrite what it means to be beautiful. We're not chasing after elusive ideals; we're challenging the myth, reclaiming beauty as something genuine, rich with character, quirks, and flaws.

Social media can feel like a glossy parade, each post a carefully constructed highlight reel. But we're here to disrupt that parade, sharing the messy, unpolished moments that make up the true story of our lives. No more filters, no more masks—just real life, unscripted.

Superficiality tempts us to believe that happiness lies in picture-perfect appearances, in magazine-cover smiles. But real beauty isn't manufactured. It's in our laughter lines, our scars, and our stories—the details that make us, us.

Imagine a world trapped in the echoes of magazine-cover perfection, where real stories are silenced by edited versions of reality. We're done with the glossy narrative. We're tearing down the cover shots and making room for stories that speak to the heart, not just to the eye.

Superficiality is the art of reducing complex emotions to emojis, of simplifying depth into symbols. But we're here to go beyond the superficial shorthand, using words and actions that reflect the true depth of our human experience.

Life's runway isn't for those who conform to fleeting trends. We're here to walk our own runway, wearing authenticity like a statement piece, telling a story with every step, free from the need to fit into society's shifting standards.

In the face of unrealistic standards, superficiality sets the benchmark for worth so low it barely holds substance. We're done inflating ourselves to meet impossible standards. Real self-worth comes from embracing who we are, not who we're told we should be.

Our scars, quirks, and laughter lines are the bold strokes on the canvas of our lives. In a world of superficial selfies, we're capturing something more lasting—the moments, flaws, and emotions that make us real, that tell our story beyond the surface.

Imagine a masquerade where everyone wears the same mask, stuck in the superficial echo chamber. We're here to disrupt that chamber with a new song, one that celebrates difference, depth, and the vibrant diversity of real human experience.

So let's raise our banner in this rebellion against superficiality, and let our anthem ring out: Authenticity over perfection. Real over retouched. Beautifully flawed over flawlessly edited. Together, let's forge a world where we celebrate the messy, the raw, and the magnificently real—where authenticity shines brighter than the gloss of superficiality.

The Validation Revelation

Let go of waiting for validation and give yourself permission to live authentically. This isn't a walk in the park; it's an exhilarating ride through the boundaries of self-limitation and a challenge to break free from the chains of approval-seeking.

The permission slips we seek often come wrapped in expectations of external validation. But it's time to tear them up and recognize that your worth isn't defined by someone else's stamp of approval. The imagined gatekeepers that you think control your path? They're illusions. You are the only one with the authority to unlock the doors to your dreams.

Permission-seeking is a comfortable trap, a buffer between you and the unknown. But life is not lived on the sidelines. It's lived out on the high wire, without a net and with full commitment. Embrace the thrill of venturing beyond the safe confines of approval.

The need for permission is like an invisible anchor that keeps you in the shallow waters of conformity. It pulls you back just as you start to reach for something deeper and more meaningful. Real growth comes when you break that anchor and allow yourself to explore freely, without waiting for someone else to say "Go."

Creativity doesn't thrive on boundaries; it thrives when we allow ourselves to think without restrictions. Give yourself the green light to imagine, create, and experiment without asking, "Is this okay?" Creativity needs no permission; it needs only space to breathe.

When you stop waiting for permission, you free yourself from self-imposed limitations. It's like cutting the tethers that kept you grounded. Spread your wings without fear, and take flight on your own terms.

The act of granting yourself permission is an act of love. It's a statement that your ideas, dreams, and quirks are not just valid but deserving of pursuit. Rather than seeking love and approval from others, turn that compassion inward and let it be the fuel that drives you.

Waiting for "the right moment" is a mirage we cling to as a way to postpone our desires. There is no perfect time. The right moment is simply when you decide to act. Tear up the permission slip that says you need to wait for an ideal set of circumstances—create your own opportunity instead.

Often, our need for permission is rooted in a fear of rejection. But rejection is simply part of the journey, a momentary obstacle rather than a stopping point. Break free from the fear that others must approve your path for it to be valid.

In a world that values conformity, granting yourself permission is a revolutionary act. It's a declaration that you refuse to be molded by outside pressures and are here to chart your own course, guided by your inner compass.

True freedom is permission-less. It's the joy of living for yourself, making choices that feel right to you without worrying about fitting in. When you live permission-free, every day becomes an expression of who you truly are.

The irony of permission-seeking is that it often limits you more than it liberates you. By letting go of the need for permission, you cut through these invisible limitations, freeing yourself to move with courage and conviction.

Expectations come pre-packaged with permission slips that often tell us to act in certain ways. But life isn't a test where you fill in the blanks according to someone else's answer key. It's a choose-your-own adventure with limitless possibilities.

Life is constantly evolving, and so are you. Give yourself permission to change, to grow, and to become who you're meant to be. Tear up any slips that insist you must remain the same, and let each new chapter of your life bring a fresh start.

Happiness shouldn't be held back by someone else's endorsement. Give yourself permission to enjoy your life fully, without waiting for anyone else to validate your joy. You are your own best advocate.

The journey to self-acceptance is ongoing, a beautifully unfinished masterpiece. Allow yourself to be incomplete, to be a work in progress. Release the pressure of perfectionism and let the true, imperfect you emerge.

This revolution against self-limitations begins when you tear up the need for permission. Step fully into your life, unscripted and unfiltered. Let go of validation, for your existence is more than enough on its own. In this grand performance of life, let your anthem ring clear: "No Permission Needed." The stage is yours—step into the spotlight, unapologetically you.

The Eternal Now

Let's cast off the shackles of the ticking clock and enter a realm where the present moment reigns supreme—the Eternal Now. Here, time isn't a relentless taskmaster, but an open invitation to savor the fullness of each heartbeat, each breath, each fleeting second.

Forget the idea that time is a line, pushing us forward without pause. In the Eternal Now, past and future merge into the richness of this single, brilliant moment. Life is not a series of scheduled tasks, but an unscripted masterpiece unfolding in real-time.

Imagine the present as a canvas that welcomes every experience, unfiltered by regrets of the past or fears of the future. Let spontaneity be your brush, painting each moment with authenticity, letting the story reveal itself without the constraints of a ticking clock.

The idea that "there's never enough time" is one of life's most convincing illusions. In reality, time is expansive, elastic, ready to stretch for the things that truly matter. When we dive fully into the present, we find a freedom that schedules can't contain, a freedom that doesn't live on a calendar but in the rhythm of our own heartbeat.

Picture a world where clocks are obsolete, where each second stretches into infinity. There's no pressure to squeeze joy into designated time slots or to fit meaning into the daily agenda. Instead, each moment becomes its own vast, boundless playground.

Rushing through life serves no one. Let's rebel against the compulsion to hurry and instead savor the pace of the present. Each moment is a delicacy; let it linger, let it sink in, let it become a part of you.

Creativity flourishes when it's untethered from deadlines and expectations. Inspiration doesn't obey a schedule; it arrives when we are open, ready, and present. The Eternal Now is the ground in which creativity roots itself deeply, drawing from the here and now to create something timeless.

The fear of running out of time—one of life's deepest anxieties—dissolves in the Now. When we fully embrace this moment, time itself feels limitless. Each heartbeat, each breath becomes a treasure, a note in the symphony of your life's song.

Relationships blossom when we meet each other here, in this space beyond schedules and agendas. True connection doesn't thrive on a clock's demands; it grows organically, like a flower opening to the sun.

Freedom is found in the present. Our wings stretch widest not in the rigid framework of a calendar but in the openness of now. Every moment in the Eternal Now is a step outside the confines of ordinary time, a step into a timeless adventure where every experience has room to breathe.

The notion that we're "too late" for anything is a fiction, a myth spun by those bound to the clock. Opportunities are always unfolding in the Eternal Now, where beginnings and endings lose their edges, blending into a perpetual opening for what comes next.

Mindfulness is a masterpiece painted on the canvas of the Now. Every distraction, every pull away from the present moment, is a pull away from life's richest colors. Let each brushstroke of the present fill your experience with presence and vitality.

Our fantasies of time travel can be tempting, yet they distract us from the beauty of where we are. The Eternal Now is the most captivating destination there is—where past, present, and future become one, where memories and dreams flow together into this singular, lived experience.

Picture the clock as a mere prop in the grand theater of your life. It has its place but doesn't dictate the drama of your journey. Instead, let the present be the scene where you rise to the fullness of your potential, fully aware, fully here.

Growth is not a sprint to the future but a constant unfolding in the gymnasium of the Now. Every present moment is a weight to lift, a lesson to learn, a triumph to celebrate.

Rebel against the need to be somewhere else, sometime else. Instead, sink into the Now, where everything you need and everything you are becomes clear. This is not just a moment; it's the journey and the destination, the anthem of your existence, timeless and unbounded.

Let the present moment be your eternal anthem—sing it with all your heart.

Embracing the eternal now is akin to stepping into a river where time flows, not linearly, but in a mesmerizing dance around you. Here, in the heart of the present, we uncover the profound truth that life's essence is not measured by the ticking of a clock but by the depth of the moments we inhabit fully. This realization is not just a philosophical musing; it's a call to action, a directive to immerse ourselves completely in the fabric of now.

- **The Illusion of Time**   Recognize that the conventional perception of time as a linear progression from past to future is a mental construct. Instead, see time as a series of present moments, each fully capable of holding the vastness of life's experiences.
- **Mindful Presence**   Cultivate a practice of mindfulness, where each task, conversation, and thought is approached with full attention. By being fully present, you transform

mundane activities into profound experiences, enriching your life with depth and meaning.

- **Joy in Spontaneity**   Break free from the rigidity of schedules and embrace spontaneity. Let the joy of unplanned moments guide your day. It's in these spaces of freedom that creativity and happiness often flourish, revealing the beauty of living unbounded by the clock.
- **Savoring Moments**   Slow down and savor each experience, whether it's a simple meal, a walk in the park, or a conversation with a loved one. By fully engaging with the present, you deepen your connection to life, finding richness in simplicity.
- **Letting Go of Fear**   Release the fear of not having enough time. In the eternal now, every moment is an opportunity, a space for action, reflection, and growth. Understand that time is not running out; it's unfolding in an endless series of nows.
- **Nurturing Relationships**   Invest in relationships with the understanding that the most precious gift you can offer is your presence. Quality time spent in the company of loved ones is infinitely more valuable than any measure of time spent distracted or disengaged.
- **Freedom from Calendars**   Challenge the tyranny of calendars and to-do lists by prioritizing activities that bring you joy and fulfillment. While planning is necessary, ensure it serves your wellbeing, not the other way around.
- **Embracing Agelessness**   View life through the lens of the eternal now, where age is irrelevant to your capacity for wonder, learning, and joy. Let your spirit be guided by curiosity and resilience, defying the societal constraints on age and time.
- **Seizing Opportunities**   Understand that it's never too late to pursue dreams, change paths, or start anew. The eternal

now is a field ripe with potential, where every moment is a fresh start, a new opportunity to craft the life you desire.
- **Living Mindfully**   Make each decision, each action, and each thought a testament to your commitment to the now. This doesn't mean forsaking the future but recognizing that the foundation for tomorrow is laid in the mindfulness of today.

Action Plan and Activities

- **Daily Mindfulness Meditation**   Dedicate time each morning or evening to meditate, focusing solely on your breath and the sensations of the present moment. This practice grounds you in the now, enhancing your awareness throughout the day.
- **Gratitude Journaling**   At the end of each day, write down three things you were grateful for. This encourages a focus on the positive moments of the day, anchoring you in the present.
- **The "One Task" Experiment**   For one week, commit to doing one task at a time, giving it your full attention. Notice the difference in the quality of your work and your mental state.
- **Technology Sabbatical**   Allocate one day a week as a technology-free day, or set specific hours each day without digital devices. Observe how this affects your engagement with the present moment.
- **Nature Walks**   Regularly spend time in nature, observing the details of the environment around you. Use all your senses to fully experience the moment, fostering a deep connection with the now.

In the eternal now, every breath, every heartbeat, is a symphony of existence played in real-time. The art of living becomes a masterful dance where we are fully awake, alive, and attuned to the richness of each moment. Let us embrace this rebellion against the tyranny of time, discovering in the process that the true essence of life is not in how many moments we capture but in how deeply we are captivated by each moment.

The Boundless Present

Imagine standing in the center of a vast, timeless expanse, where past regrets and future anxieties dissolve into the immediacy of the present moment. This is the Eternal Now—a realm where life unfolds not in fragments but in its entirety, inviting us to live fully, deeply, and authentically. The Eternal Now is not just an idea; it's a practice, a way of being that transforms how we experience time, purpose, and presence.

The "NOW" Framework for Living Fully

To immerse yourself in the Eternal Now, use the NOW framework:

1. **N – Notice the Moment:** Cultivate awareness by observing your surroundings, sensations, and emotions without judgment.
2. **O – Open to Experience:** Embrace each moment with curiosity, whether it brings joy, challenge, or stillness.
3. **W – Weave Presence into Action:** Approach each task, conversation, or thought with undivided attention, making the ordinary extraordinary.

The Mindfulness Ladder
1. **Base Rung – Awareness:** Start by noticing the present moment, focusing on your breath, the sounds around you, or the sensations in your body.
2. **Middle Rung – Engagement:** Deepen your connection by fully engaging with whatever you're doing—listening, working, or simply being.
3. **Top Rung – Gratitude:** Conclude each day by reflecting on the moments that brought joy, meaning, or insight, solidifying your connection to the now.

Life is like a river, with time flowing ceaselessly. Most of us stand on the banks, anxiously watching the current. The Eternal Now invites us to step into the river, feeling the water flow around us. In this immersion, we find clarity, peace, and a profound connection to the rhythm of life.

Imagine your life as a symphony where each present moment is a note. Instead of rushing to reach the finale, savor the unfolding melody. Every note, whether quiet or bold, contributes to the beauty of the whole.

Journaling Prompts: Anchoring in the Now
- What does it feel like to be fully present? Reflect on a recent moment when you felt truly immersed in the present.
- Identify one recurring distraction that pulls you out of the now. How can you address it mindfully?
- List three simple activities that bring you into the present moment, and commit to doing one today.

Visualization Exercise: Entering the Eternal Now
- Close your eyes and picture yourself stepping into a sunlit meadow where time seems to pause. Feel the warmth of the

sun, hear the rustling leaves, and breathe deeply. In this space, there are no deadlines or worries—only the fullness of now. Let this vision guide you throughout your day, helping you return to presence whenever distractions arise.

Shift your focus from chasing goals or moments to savoring what's already here. The Eternal Now teaches us that life's richness isn't found in "what's next" but in fully embracing "what's now."

Time feels scarce when we rush, yet it expands when we immerse ourselves in the present. Embracing the Eternal Now reveals that the depth of each moment matters more than its duration.

Daily Practices for Presence
1. **Morning Grounding Ritual:** Begin each day with a few minutes of mindfulness—breathing deeply and setting an intention to stay present.
2. **Mindful Meals:** Eat one meal a day in silence, focusing on the flavors, textures, and sensations of each bite.
3. **Single-Tasking:** Dedicate yourself fully to one task at a time, whether it's writing an email or folding laundry, and notice how it feels to give it your complete attention.

Breaking Free from the Clock
1. **Clock-Free Hours:** Designate a few hours each day where you ignore clocks and simply follow your natural rhythm.
2. **The Pause Practice:** Before transitioning between tasks, pause for a few breaths to fully appreciate the moment you're in.

Every moment spent in the Eternal Now is a victory over the tyranny of time. Celebrate your ability to pause, breathe, and truly live. Recognize that each present moment is a brushstroke in the masterpiece of your life.

The Eternal Now isn't just a place—it's a way of living. When you embrace it, you discover that life's richest treasures are found not in what's ahead but in what's here.

Living in the Eternal Now leaves a legacy not of haste but of harmony. Your presence inspires others to slow down, savor, and find meaning in the present.

In the stillness of now, we uncover the infinite. Let each moment be a testament to your capacity to live deeply and authentically, painting your life with the colors of presence and joy.

4-Week Action Plan for Harmony in the Chaos: Cultivating Depth, Balance, and Resonance in Life's Symphony

Congratulations on completing "Harmony in the Chaos," the second part of "Embrace Chaos, Find Purpose." This journey has taken you through the complexities and nuances of balancing the multifaceted aspects of your life while cultivating depth and resonance within your personal and professional spheres. You've explored how to weave the intricate tapestry of relationships, navigate the ever-changing landscape of life's challenges, and march confidently into the chaos with purpose and integrity.

As you move forward, remember that each chapter you've encountered serves as a guidepost, offering strategies, reflections, and insights to help you achieve a more harmonious existence. The path to balance and depth is ongoing, a dynamic dance that evolves with every step you take. To ensure these insights become integrated parts of your journey, we invite you to revisit the chapters for further exploration and to deepen your engagement with the concepts presented.

To bridge the gap between understanding and application, we've crafted a four-week action plan. This plan is your roadmap to applying the lessons learned, designed to foster growth, encourage self-reflection, and empower you to create a life that resonates with your deepest values and aspirations. It's your guide to transforming the chaos into a symphony of purposeful action.

Week 1 Action Plan: Laying Foundations for Harmony

As you embark on the journey to cultivate depth, balance, and resonance in your life's symphony, the first week is about setting the stage for transformative growth. Let's dive into actionable steps and reflections drawn from the initial chapters of "Book 2, Harmony in the Chaos."

Day 1: The Garden of Priorities
- **Activity:** Create your Garden of Priorities. List your current top five priorities on paper, then assess if they genuinely reflect your values and the life you wish to lead.
- **Reflection:** Consider the soil of your garden—is it nourishing your priorities, or is it time to re-till and plant anew?

Day 2: The Tapestry of Relationships
- **Activity:** Identify the key threads in your Tapestry of Relationships. Reach out to at least one person who strengthens your tapestry with joy, support, or wisdom.
- **Reflection:** Reflect on the diversity of threads in your tapestry—are there colors missing, or threads that no longer serve you?

Day 3: The Catalyst for Change
- **Activity:** Embrace one small change today that can act as a catalyst for larger transformation. This could be a new habit, breaking an old pattern, or making a decision you've been postponing.
- **Reflection:** How did initiating this change make you feel? Empowered, anxious, excited?

Day 4: Beyond the Shallows
- **Activity:** Dedicate at least 30 minutes to an activity that deepens your understanding or skills in a particular area of interest. This could be reading, a creative endeavor, or learning a new skill.
- **Reflection:** Explore how diving deeper into this area can add richness and depth to your life's symphony.

Day 5: The Map of Purpose
- **Activity:** Draft a basic map of your life's current path. Include your passions, dreams, and goals. Highlight areas where you feel off-course.
- **Reflection:** Contemplate the roads taken and not taken. How does this map guide you towards your true purpose?

Day 6: Calibrating Your Moral Compass
- **Activity:** Reflect on a recent decision. Was it aligned with your moral compass? Write down thoughts or feelings that influenced your decision-making process.
- **Reflection:** Consider the alignment of your moral compass. Does it need recalibration to better reflect your authentic self?

Day 7: Avoiding the Temptation of Drift
- **Activity:** Identify areas of your life where you're merely drifting. Set one actionable goal to regain direction and momentum.
- **Reflection:** Reflect on the forces that cause you to drift. How can you better anchor yourself in purposeful action?

Week 1 Closing Reflection:

At the end of this week, take a moment to reflect on the foundational work you've begun. Harmony in life's chaos doesn't arrive overnight, but each step you've taken this week is a note in the right direction. How do you feel about the path unfolding before you? What insights have emerged from this week's activities and reflections?

Remember, the journey to harmony is uniquely yours. Embrace the chaos, dance with complexity, and cultivate a life symphony that resonates with depth, balance, and authenticity. Continue to build on these foundations as you progress through the next weeks of transformative action.

Week 2 Action Plan: Deepening Connections and Embracing Change

As we move into the second week of "Harmony in the Chaos," our focus shifts towards deepening our connections and embracing the inevitable changes life presents. This week's activities and reflections are designed to strengthen your tapestry of relationships and navigate through life's transformations with grace.

Day 8: Storms of Distractions

- **Activity:** Identify your main sources of distraction and commit to a two-hour block where you consciously avoid them. Use this time to engage in a focused activity that contributes to your goals.
- **Reflection:** How did the absence of these distractions affect your focus and productivity? What did you learn about your distraction triggers?

Day 9: Rogue Waves

- **Activity:** Reflect on a recent "rogue wave" event in your life—an unexpected challenge that caught you off guard. Write down how you responded and what you might do differently next time.

- **Reflection:** How can preparing for life's rogue waves make you more resilient and adaptable?

Day 10: Beyond the Known
- **Activity:** Step out of your comfort zone today. Try something new that challenges you, whether it's a new skill, a conversation with a stranger, or a different route to work.
- **Reflection:** Explore the feelings and outcomes from stepping beyond the known. Did this experience reveal anything new about yourself?

Day 11: The Art of Reflection
- **Activity:** Dedicate 30 minutes to silent reflection. Contemplate where you are in life, where you want to go, and what might be holding you back.
- **Reflection:** What insights emerged from this quiet reflection? How can these insights guide your steps moving forward?

Day 12: Tools of Wisdom
- **Activity:** Seek out a new tool of wisdom—a book, podcast, or seminar that aligns with your goals for growth and learning. Spend at least an hour engaging with this new resource.
- **Reflection:** What wisdom did you uncover, and how can it be applied to your journey towards harmony and balance?

Day 13: Where Mavericks Reign
- **Activity:** Embrace your inner maverick. Do one thing today that breaks from convention but feels authentic to you.
- **Reflection:** How did it feel to act on your maverick instincts? What does this tell you about the balance between conformity and authenticity in your life?

Day 14: Weathering Emotional Storms
- **Activity:** Think of an emotional storm you're currently navigating. Write down strategies you're using or could use to weather it with resilience.
- **Reflection:** Reflect on the strength and wisdom gained from weathering past emotional storms. How do these experiences fortify you for current and future challenges?

Week 2 Closing Reflection:

Reflect on the progress you've made in deepening your connections and embracing change. This week was about pushing boundaries, seeking wisdom, and learning to navigate through life's unpredictable waves with a maverick spirit. Consider how these experiences are weaving new patterns into your tapestry of relationships and shaping your journey through the chaos.

What lessons stood out most vividly? How have these activities and reflections helped you move closer to achieving harmony in the chaos? Carry these insights forward as you continue to cultivate depth, balance, and resonance in your life's symphony.

Week 3 Action Plan: Embracing Integrity and Liberating Choices

In the third week of "Harmony in the Chaos," we'll focus on embracing our inner integrity and liberating our choices. This journey involves recognizing our core values, challenging our comfort zones, and embracing your inner rebel. Here's your guide to unlocking the next level of depth, balance, and resonance in your life's symphony.

Day 15: Your Inner Scholar

- **Activity:** Dedicate an hour to learning something new that aligns with your interests or goals. This could be through a book, online course, or documentary.
- **Reflection:** How does continuous learning enrich your life and support your journey toward authenticity and resilience?

Day 16: Embrace Your Inner Rebel

- **Activity:** Identify one societal expectation that doesn't align with your true self. Today, consciously choose to rebel against this norm in a small, personal way.
- **Reflection:** Reflect on the liberation that comes from not conforming. How can embracing your inner rebel lead to a more authentic life?

Day 17: Liberate Your Choices
- **Activity:** Think of a decision you've been postponing because you're worried about others' opinions. Make that choice today, based solely on what's best for you.
- **Reflection:** How does it feel to make decisions based on your own needs and desires rather than external expectations?

Day 18: The Dance of Integrity
- **Activity:** Write down three core values that are most important to you. For each, list a way you can more fully integrate these values into your daily life.
- **Reflection:** How does living in alignment with your core values impact your sense of self and your interactions with others?

Day 19: The Jar of Careful Choices
- **Activity:** Create a physical or digital Jar of Careful Choices. Whenever you find yourself stressing over something insignificant, write it down and "put" it in the jar as a way to let it go.
- **Reflection:** At the end of the day, review the contents of your Jar of Careful Choices. How many of your worries were truly worth the energy you gave them?

Day 20: Your Most Potent Sorcery
- **Activity:** Identify a talent or skill that you often take for granted. Find a way to share or celebrate this "sorcery" with others today.
- **Reflection:** How does acknowledging and sharing your unique talents contribute to your sense of authenticity and purpose?

Day 21: The Comfort Zone
- **Activity:** Step outside your comfort zone in a significant way. This could be initiating a difficult conversation, trying a new activity, or exploring a place you've never been.
- **Reflection:** What did you learn about yourself by stepping outside your comfort zone? How can pushing these boundaries fuel your growth?

Week 3 Closing Reflection:

This week was about tapping into our inner scholar, embracing the rebel within, and making choices that reflect our true selves. Each day's activity and reflection were steps toward a more integrated, authentic existence, challenging us to live in alignment with our deepest values and to explore the edges of our comfort zones.

Reflect on the shifts in your perspective and behavior over the past week. How have these actions and reflections helped you to see yourself and your place in the world differently? What insights will you carry forward as you continue to cultivate a harmonious symphony of depth, balance, and resonance in your life?

Embrace these lessons as you prepare for the final week of our journey through "Harmony in the Chaos," where we'll confront procrastination, address the busyness epidemic, and explore the eternal now.

Week 4 Action Plan: Conquering Procrastination and Embracing the Moment

In our final week of "Harmony in the Chaos," we delve into the art of conquering procrastination, challenging the busyness epidemic, and embracing the eternal now. This phase is dedicated to actionable strategies that encourage us to live more fully in each moment, prioritize what truly matters, and cultivate a life of purpose and depth.

Day 22: The Procrastination Dragon
- **Activity:** Identify one task you've been procrastinating on. Break it down into smaller, manageable steps. Tackle the first step today using the Triple Sprint Method (20-minute sprints, followed by a 15-minute rejuvenating break).
- **Reflection:** Reflect on the barriers that have been holding you back from completing this task. How does addressing procrastination directly change your approach to challenges?

Day 23: Purpose is not a Unicorn
- **Activity:** Spend time today defining or refining your purpose. Write a mission statement for your life that includes your passions, values, and the impact you wish to have.

- **Reflection:** How does having a clear sense of purpose guide your decisions and actions? In what ways does it serve as a compass during times of uncertainty?

Day 24: March Headlong into the Chaos
- **Activity:** Choose an area of your life currently in chaos. Instead of avoiding it, confront it head-on with a plan to bring order or understanding to the situation.
- **Reflection:** How does facing chaos directly, rather than avoiding it, provide you with a sense of empowerment and resilience?

Day 25: The Busyness Epidemic
- **Activity:** Conduct a time audit of your day to identify periods spent on unproductive busyness. Choose one activity to eliminate or reduce, reallocating that time to something more meaningful.
- **Reflection:** How does reducing busyness affect your stress levels and overall satisfaction? What benefits do you notice from reallocating time to activities that align with your purpose?

Day 26: The Theatre of Judgement
- **Activity:** Reflect on a recent situation where you felt judged by others. Write a letter to yourself from the perspective of a compassionate observer, offering support and understanding.
- **Reflection:** How does changing your perspective on judgment help you to cultivate a stronger sense of self-compassion and resilience?

Day 27: The Photoshop Rebellion
- **Activity:** Identify an aspect of your life or self-image you've been "photoshopping" for the sake of others. Commit to

one action that celebrates this aspect authentically, without alteration or apology.
- **Reflection:** What does rebelling against the pressure to present a "photoshopped" version of yourself reveal about your values and the importance of authenticity?

Day 28: The Eternal Now

- **Activity:** Practice mindfulness or meditation for 15 minutes, focusing solely on the present moment. Alternatively, engage in an activity that fully absorbs your attention, bringing you into the "now."
- **Reflection:** How does embracing the eternal now impact your ability to appreciate life's moments? What shifts do you notice in your stress levels, attention, and overall wellbeing?

Week 4 Closing Reflection:

This week was a journey through confronting procrastination, challenging societal pressures, and embracing the beauty of each moment. As you reflect on the past seven days, consider the shifts in your perception and actions. How have these exercises helped you to engage more deeply with your life, prioritize effectively, and live in alignment with your authentic self?

Reflect on the entire four-week journey through "Harmony in the Chaos." What lessons have resonated most deeply with you? How will you integrate these insights into your daily life to continue cultivating depth, balance, and resonance?

As we close this chapter, remember that the quest for harmony in life's chaos is ongoing. Each day presents new opportunities to weave the threads of your existence into a tapestry of meaning and beauty. Carry forward the lessons learned, the practices adopted, and the insights gained, and let them guide you in orchestrating a life of purpose, balance, and profound impact.

Afterword for the Book

As we reach the end of this journey through the intricate landscape of self-discovery and intentional living, my heart is full of gratitude for having you here, alongside me. I hope these reflections, insights, and practices have sparked a desire within you to build a life guided by purpose, not by the pull of distractions. This book was never meant to hand you all the answers but to be a companion in the ongoing process of sculpting a life that feels truly yours.

Remember, this isn't a solitary adventure but a dance we all share, each of us adding our unique rhythm. Your distinctiveness, your quirks, and the inner vision you hold—these are the very essence of a life that leaves an imprint on the world. As you move forward, lean into your path with confidence, embrace the unknown with a sense of curiosity, and let your choices inspire others to seek their own version of fulfillment.

May you lead with a compassionate heart, an open mind, and a commitment to living in alignment with your highest values. And in those moments where you feel uncertain or discouraged, know that the life you are shaping is a testament to the intentional choices you make. This isn't a goodbye; it's a standing invitation to keep stepping forward with purpose.

Because at the end of the day, it's not about a life perfectly planned—it's about one crafted with care, with thought, and with love.

To a life well-lived and deeply felt.

With gratitude and respect,

William R. Stanek

About the Author: William R. Stanek

Meet the Visionary, the Storyteller, and Your Guide on the Journey to Intentional Living

Biography

William R. Stanek is no ordinary author in the world of personal growth. With a background that's woven with more experiences than can be counted, Stanek is known for his straightforward wisdom, practical insights, and a talent for helping others build lives that align with their core values. His work speaks to those who seek authenticity and a real connection to their purpose, bringing an inspiring yet realistic approach to the journey of self-discovery.

Throughout his journey, Stanek has played many roles—teacher, innovator, mentor, and artist—each experience adding to the perspective he shares in his books. He is known for being the voice people turn to when conventional advice falls short and when what's needed isn't a quick fix but a path to meaningful change. Over his career, he has helped countless individuals rethink their relationship with success, personal growth, and what it truly means to live a purposeful life.

As a leader and technologist at the intersection of business, technology, and leadership, William's work extends far beyond the written word. He has spent years inspiring action, driving meaningful change, and guiding others on how to create impact that resonates, endures, and honors each individual's unique journey. His influence spans professions and walks of life, providing a grounding perspective in a world that often encourages us to chase everything at once. In this book,

William shares his experiences, insights, and deep conviction in the power of intentional living with a broader audience.

Connect with William R. Stanek

Join William in exploring new ideas, challenging conventional wisdom, and pushing the boundaries of what's possible in personal growth. Connect with him here:

LinkedIn: Follow William for updates, articles, and perspectives on intentional living and personal growth.

https://www.linkedin.com/in/williamstanek/

Facebook: Like his author page for daily insights, reflections, and updates.

http://www.facebook.com/William.Stanek.Author

Twitter: Follow for thought-provoking tweets and personal growth tips in 280 characters.

http://www.twitter.com/WilliamStanek

Website: Visit http://www.williamrstanek.com to learn more about his books, workshops, and other projects.

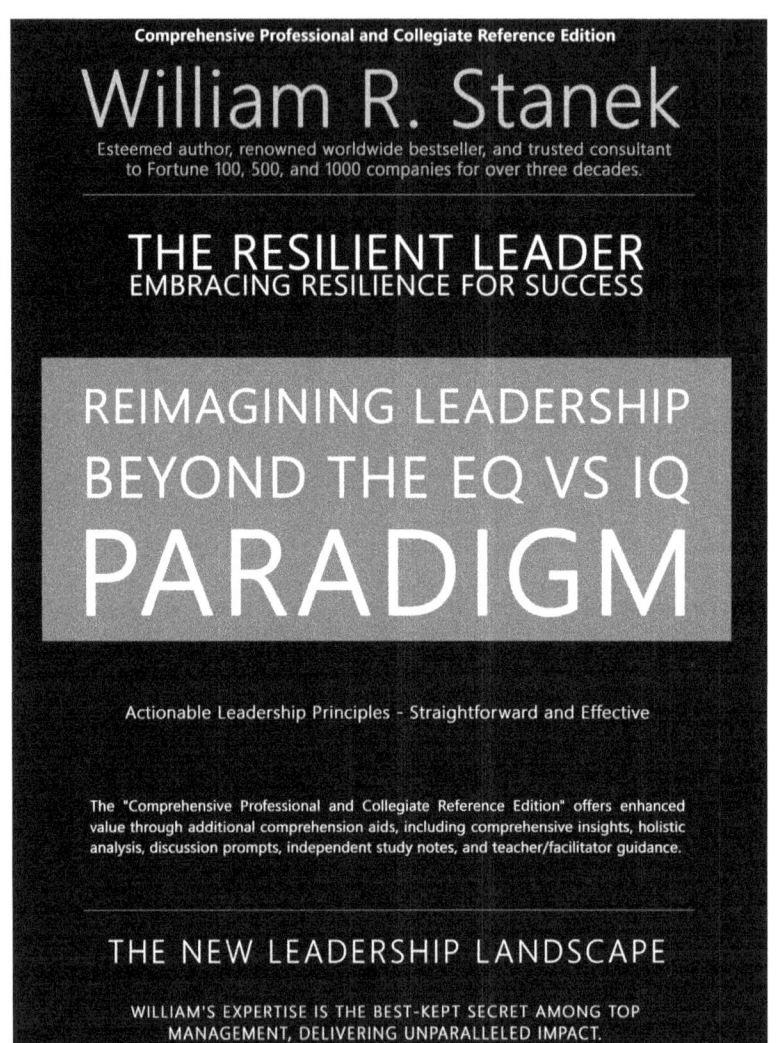

"The Resilient Leader, Embracing Resilience for Success" stands out in the crowded landscape of leadership and emotional intelligence books by offering a fresh, holistic approach to leadership that transcends traditional models. This groundbreaking work by William R. Stanek redefines the essence of effective leadership in the modern era, distinguishing itself through several key differentiators:

- **Holistic Integration of Multiple Intelligences**   While most leadership books focus on emotional intelligence (EQ) or traditional cognitive intelligence (IQ), "The Resilient Leader, Embracing Resilience for Success" introduces readers to the 8 Pillars of Leadership. This innovative framework encompasses Emotional Resilience, Creative Intelligence, Practical Intelligence, Cultural Intelligence, Intrapersonal Intelligence, Interpersonal Intelligence, Ethical Intelligence, and Analytical Intelligence. By embracing a broader spectrum of intelligences, the book equips leaders with a multifaceted toolkit, enabling them to navigate the complexities of the contemporary landscape more effectively than ever before.

- **Emphasis on Emotional Resilience**   "The Resilient Leader, Embracing Resilience for Success" delves deep into emotional resilience, offering readers actionable strategies to cultivate this essential trait. The book presents emotional resilience as the bedrock of leadership excellence, enabling leaders to withstand challenges, adapt to change, thrive in adversity, and so much more. Whereas most literature on emotional intelligence or emotional resilience treats resilience as a narrow set of traits or a subset of emotional intelligence, "The Resilient Leader, Embracing Resilience for Success" reconceptualizes it as a multifaceted intelligence in its own right. This book goes far beyond the typical definitions and presents emotional resilience as a complex, dynamic intelligence that is critical for effective leadership.

- **Rigorous Self-Assessment Tool**   Distinct from other leadership books that offer generalized advice, "The Resilient Leader, Embracing Resilience for Success" integrates a cutting-edge self-assessment tool. This personalized assessment allows readers to evaluate their strengths and areas for growth, providing a tailored roadmap for personal and professional development. This actionable, data-driven approach ensures that readers can make concrete progress on their leadership journey.

- **Case Studies and Real-World Application**   While many books on leadership and emotional intelligence rely on theoretical principles, "The Resilient Leader, Embracing Resilience for Success" grounds its insights in practical reality. Through a series of detailed case studies featuring real-world scenarios and leadership challenges, the book illustrates how the principles of resilient leadership can be applied in various contexts. From crisis management in the financial sector to navigating complex mergers and leading through global pandemics, these case studies offer readers a window into the transformative power of resilient leadership in action.

- **Future-Oriented Leadership Vision**   Stanek's book critically examines the evolution of leadership theories and practices, from ancient times through the industrial revolution to the present day, offering a visionary outlook on the future of leadership. Unlike books that dwell on past or current leadership models, "The Resilient Leader, Embracing Resilience for Success" charts a course for the future, advocating for a comprehensive, adaptable leadership approach that meets the demands of an ever-changing world. This forward-thinking perspective encourages leaders to not only adapt to the new normal but to thrive within it, paving the way for a new era of leadership excellence.

In summary, "The Resilient Leader, Embracing Resilience for Success" offers a unique, comprehensive guide that goes beyond traditional leadership tenets, providing readers with the insights and tools needed to excel in today's dynamic environment. By combining a holistic view of intelligence, a focus on emotional resilience, practical tools for self-assessment, real-world applicability, and a visionary leadership approach, this book is an essential resource for anyone looking to lead effectively in the 21st century.

www.ingramcontent.com/pod-product-compliance
Lightning Source LLC
Chambersburg PA
CBHW071855160426
43209CB00005B/1062